WILLIAMS
SONOMA
CALIFORNIA

Newlywed Entertaining

PHOTOGRAPHY BY JOHN KERNICK

weldon**owen**

classic appeal
Roast Chicken with Potatoes & Carrots
(recipe page 127) is a welcome addition
to your table any night of the year.

Contents

holiday celebrations

cocktail parties

Colorful cocktails and
fresh, vibrant food like this
Mediterranean Flatbread
(recipe page 108) set a
convivial scene.

Sharing Your Home

Throwing a party together as newlyweds gives you a chance to welcome people into your home as a couple, to share the love with them that they have given to you throughout the wedding process, and to start new traditions, including hosting holidays. It's a great way to put some of your favorite tableware and serving pieces to work, too. Over time, you'll establish a look and feel for your parties that set them apart from everyone else's.

Like marriage, entertaining today isn't tied to old rules. Dinner parties don't have to be sit-down affairs; a kitchen party or gathering on the back deck works just as well. Cocktail parties don't have to be catered affairs with hired bartenders; you can pass a signature cocktail or two or set up a craft bar. Instead of served hors d'oeuvres, gather around big platters with everyone talking, laughing, and reaching for food all at once. A do-it-yourself approach can lead to some of the best events: a taco bar, make-your-own pizza night, a frittata free-for-all. And mix up your good china and crystal with everyday dishes and assorted flatware for a style statement that's all your own.

In fact, mixing and matching to create your own party vibe is at the heart of this book, which is organized around types of occasions rather than strict menus. From daytime brunches and lunches to alfresco barbecues and picnics, to dressier dinners, holidays, and cocktail parties, there's inspiration for any event. You can focus on one dish, pick and choose several that appeal to you, or use one of the suggested menus in the back of the book. Scattered throughout are tips and ideas for serving and presentation, table settings, drinks, cooking techniques, and shortcuts to make entertaining easier. The goal is to make the party as fun for you as it is for your guests, because *that* is the secret recipe for entertaining success.

Decisions, Decisions

Now, with your partner by your side and a well-stocked kitchen, it's time to have a party, especially with two groups of friends and colleagues to enjoy. So that's your first decision: whom to invite. It could be best friends, couples you've known forever or recently met, out-of-towners, colleagues, family, neighbors, book clubbers, new faces, or an eclectic (but not random) mix. Who knows? You might matchmake the next newlyweds.

CURATE THE MIX Keep in mind a balance of personalities. An outgoing person is an asset at a party, helping take the pressure off the hosts for keeping conversation going, but good listeners and people with interests in common are important, too, as well as people with divergent jobs, lifestyles, or hobbies. Think about a mix of ages and experience, people further along in their careers or retired, and people just starting out or still in graduate school. If someone is really shy—or really outgoing—assign them the task of passing food or pouring drinks. The more everyone mingles, the more conversation will flow.

CHOOSE A PARTY STYLE Once you know who is on the invite list, you can decide the style of the party. If it is your inner circle, you can do anything—casual and spontaneous. If it is the boss and her partner, a more elegant dinner party may be appropriate. For holidays, decide if you are going to blend your family traditions or carve out new territory. Mix it up with a weekend brunch or lunch, a midweek gathering for drinks and appetizers, or an end-of-week sit-down dinner. Each party style suggests its own approach to decor, seating, and indoor-outdoor possibilities.

CHECK THE CALENDAR Pick a date that works for you. That may seem obvious, but you'd be surprised how hard it is to schedule something that works for everyone. Although Saturday night might be tempting because you have that day free to prepare and the next to recover, you might consider times that are less predictable, but equally welcome. How about a Sunday lunch, Tuesday cocktails, Wednesday spaghetti feed, or Friday night barbecue?

SEND OUT INVITATIONS People love written invitations, especially for formal occasions such as holidays, graduations, and anniversaries, but digital invitations are definitely acceptable. Match the invitation to the party style, and be creative. Check out websites for predesigned invitation templates and apps for designing your own. For most parties, invite guests two to three weeks in advance (more than three weeks and they tend to forget). For last-minute affairs and casual dinner, a day or two's notice can work.

crafting the menu

Now the fun part: you get to put your heads together on what to serve. Luckily, the season will do a lot of the work for you, showcasing the best food choices and methods of the moment: braises and sautés for the tender foods of spring; grilled, raw, and chilled foods during summer; soups and layered dishes in autumn; and cozy stews and baked dishes in winter. The recipes in this book will give you ideas for any time of year as well as ways to vary them with the seasons.

keep it fresh
Show off beautiful
ingredients in easy
seasonal recipes like
Shaved Zucchini Salad
with Lemon & Mint
(recipe page 66).

Strategies for Stress-Free Hosts

If a party is fun for the hosts, it is fun for the guests, so do everything you can to enjoy yourselves. Dividing the work between the two of you makes hosting easier, but it takes a sense of humor and a willingness to compromise to do this without conflict. Remember that you're in this together, and the more you organize, the more likely you are to have fun.

WORK AS A TEAM Start by writing down the menu, creating the shopping list, and noting everything that can be made ahead. Then prepare a timeline of what to do a week or a few days ahead, the day before, the morning of the party, an hour before, and last minute. Decide who is going to do each task, put initials next to each one so you don't forget, and post the timeline where you can both see it.

PREP AHEAD Cook ahead what you can, such as soups and stews—they taste better reheated anyway. Make sauces, salsas, and pestos that can chill for a few days. Wash and spin-dry lettuces. Chop and prep vegetables and refrigerate them in individual bags.

EVALUATE THE SPACE Make your home party-ready in advance: Move furniture, stow clutter, and clear space in the refrigerator for party food and drink. Figure out where to put guest coats and purses. Clean the guest bathroom, and set out fresh soap and towels.

INVENTORY COOKWARE Several days ahead, make sure you have the necessary pots, pans, bakeware, and tools for the menu. Buy or borrow anything you lack. Go through the same process for your barware (see page 16).

SET THE TABLE One of the easiest ways to eliminate stress is to set the table in advance. Select your platters, bowls, and serving utensils for both appetizers and the meal. Put a sticky note on each item so you remember what they will be used for. Clean off dusty glassware and polish silver.

INCLUDE FLOWERS & MUSIC A simple way to make your space festive is to buy flowers one day ahead for the table and the rest of the house, including a vase with a single stem for the bathroom. Plan a music playlist that expresses your personalities or the party theme but that doesn't overwhelm conversation. Forget about it once guests arrive; it's there for background, even if it repeats.

ready tableware

Having extra plates and flatware available is key for last-minute entertaining.

pretest recipes

If you are trying a new recipe, consider doing a dry run at least one time before you serve it at a party.

finalize the menu

What to say when guests ask "What should we bring?" If you have a vision of what you are serving from appetizers through dessert, tell them to bring only a smile. If it is a group effort and a cohesive menu is important, assign specific dishes. If they arrive with a bottle of wine, etiquette requires only a sincere thank you; you are not obligated to serve it (although it is nice to do so).

First Impressions

The minute your guests walk in, you want them to feel the mood you've created. Is it relaxed and casual, with platters of food in the kitchen or a DIY station where guests can pitch in to assemble dishes for themselves (see page 20)? Is it an elegant night, with candlelight and jazz? Is it cocktails in the living room, on the deck, or both? Is there a theme? Whatever you choose, it can tell a story about you as a couple. Here are a few pointers for all occasions.

MUSIC Have music going before anyone arrives. It gets you in a party frame of mind. With playlists and streaming devices, it's easy to pick a format and let it run the whole time. Be sure to find the right volume; people should be aware of what's playing, but only as a background layer.

LIGHTS Lighting is as much an ingredient as food. Keep electric lights low for a flattering effect, and amp up the ambience with tea lights, votives (even in the guest bathroom), string lights, lanterns, and candles.

SCENT AWARENESS You want your guests to smell the food (it stimulates hunger), so avoid highly fragrant flowers and use unscented candles (also to honor people who are scent sensitive).

COCKTAILS & SNACKS Chic at any party, cocktails can be one or two signature drinks for the night, a big-batch punch, or from a party bar (see page 16). Have lots of little salty snacks (see page 231), such as olives, nuts, cheeses, cured meats, or cheese straws. Munching on these brings a desire for a drink, which gets the good times rolling.

KITCHEN TIDINESS Seems obvious, but if you don't plan ahead and clean as you prep, you may find yourself with pots in the sink or a swishing dishwasher when people arrive, which makes guests feel like they should pitch in and help.

EXTRA GLASSES People misplace their glasses all the time, so have spares on hand (same goes for plates, flatware, and napkins). At the last minute, you may need more than you think.

set the stage

Create a magical scene with ready-to-slurp Oysters Mignonette (recipe page 167), candlelight, and succulents.

The Party Bar

As with a recipe, a cocktail is only as good as the ingredients that go into it. Shop for top-quality brands, and store bottles in a cool place, away from direct sunlight. The higher the alcohol content, the longer the shelf life, so hard liquors almost never go bad, while lower-alcohol vermouth and sherry are best stored in the refrigerator. Both the liquors and mixers listed below can be blended into mixed drinks or sipped on their own. With these, you can make classic cocktails or artisanal ones (see pages 223–227 for recipes) or concoct signature drinks of your own.

LIQUOR

Brandy or Cognac sidecar, punch, old-fashioned

Gin martini, gin and tonic, negroni

Rum, light & dark light: mojito, daiquiri dark: punch, dark and stormy

Tequila, silver margarita, paloma

Vodka Moscow mule, cosmopolitan, martini, screwdriver

Whiskey, bourbon or rye & Scotch or Irish whiskey Manhattan (bourbon), whiskey sour, old-fashioned

MIXERS

Aperol or Lillet aperitif, spritz

Amari digestif, such as Fernet-Branca

Bitters for finishing cocktails

Campari Manhattan, negroni, Americano

Cointreau margarita, cosmopolitan

Sake/Sherry saketini, cobbler, soft cocktails

Vermouth, dry and sweet dry: aperitif, dry martini, gibson sweet: Manhattan, negroni, Americano

NONALCOHOLIC

Ginger beer

Orange, grapefruit, and cranberry juices

Seltzer

Sparkling water

Tonic

the importance of ice

Ice is no longer an afterthought; it's a key ingredient in craft cocktails because the shape and size of the cube can affect the quality of the drink. Larger cubes melt slowly so flavors aren't diluted and drinks stay colder longer. Specialty shapes, including king-size cubes, ice spheres, cylindrical cubes for highballs, and custom shapes from flowers to skulls, can be frozen in silicone molds. Crushed or pebble ice is best for "tiki" drinks and juleps: wrap cubes in a clean cloth and hit them with a muddler to break them into small pieces. Freeze ingredients in ice cubes, such as blackberries or mint leaves, for extra flavor and color in the glass. For the best taste, make ice with filtered water. For cocktail parties, plan on a pound of ice per guest.

BAR TOOLS

CITRUS PRESS, ZESTING TOOLS, PARING KNIFE for squeezing juice, stripping peel, and cutting citrus slices for garnish.

COCKTAIL SHAKER & STRAINER in any of these configurations: an all-metal shaker with a tumbler, tight lid, and built-in strainer; a Boston shaker with pint-glass tumbler and metal tumbler that lock together; or a mason-jar shaker with a screw-on strainer. If your shaker does not have a built-in strainer, use a Hawthorne strainer.

CORKSCREW & BOTTLE OPENER for wine and beer.

Wine & Beer for Parties

Even if you set up a cocktail bar, many guests will still drink wine and beer. Plan on serving two kinds of red wine, two kinds of white wine, and a sparkling wine at a cocktail party or a bottle of each for drinks before dinner. For wine during dinner, pair the wine with the menu; it's meant to make the food taste even better. The style of your gathering should inform your choice of the types to have on hand.

CASUAL PARTIES

The perfect pairing of beverage to food is less of a concern when your gathering is a casual one. Choose the varietals and brews you like, put them on ice if needed, and make them easily accessible to your guests.

SOMETHING BUBBLY Champagne from France always makes a celebration, but sparkling Prosecco and Cava wines are cost-saving alternatives to cocktails and great for mixing into spritzes and bellinis (see page 44).

SOMETHING WHITE OR PINK For sipping, people love easy-drinking wines, such as Sauvignon Blanc, Chenin Blanc, Pinot Grigio, torrontés, Sancerre, and rosé. Chardonnay is heavier but still a crowd-pleaser.

SOMETHING RED Stay on the light side with reds, offering a Pinot Noir or Beaujolais that goes well with a whole range of foods.

LAGERS & ALES Offer one of each kind. Lagers are light, refreshing beers that go with anything, especially salty snacks, pickled veggies, and charcuterie. Ales are hoppier and also pair with anything but are especially tasty with cheese.

FORMAL DINNERS

Share your menu with a wine vendor you trust. They have the most knowledge about matching wine with food, and there's a world of varietals to explore.

CRISP WHITES Pair these with global foods, spicy dishes, and salty appetizers. Options include Sauvignon Blanc, Pinot Grigio, Albariño, and dry Riesling.

RICH WHITES Chardonnay, especially white Bordeaux, works with buttery, creamy dishes. Heavier fruit-forward whites, such as Gewürztraminer and Riesling, pair nicely with Asian food, as well as spicy and/or grilled preparations.

LIGHT & MEDIUM-BODIED REDS Pinot Noir is fantastic with grilled pork and lamb, vegetables, and roasted poultry. It also goes with cheeses and appetizers. Chianti and Brunello are lovely with pasta or light Italian preparations.

FULL-BODIED REDS Robust, extracted wines such as Zinfandel, Malbec, Cabernet Sauvignon, and Shiraz, as well as heartier Italian reds such as Barolo and Barbaresco, pair with steaks, beef and lamb roasts, and hearty stews.

easy pairings

The old adage about white with fish and poultry and red with meat isn't really true. It is the other elements in the dish that determine the pairing, so consider the spices, the acid, the fat content, the cooking method, and your own personal preference.

Casual & Outdoor Parties

Informal gatherings are a simpler way to entertain: It's not that the stakes are lower—it's that the effect is relaxed, with no pretense and no pressure, and you can be utterly yourselves. Ask friends and family over for a barbecue or brunch on the patio, a make-your-own panini lunch when a big game is on, a winter soup and pizza party in the kitchen, or a family-style dinner in the dining room.

TABLE SETTINGS

Casual entertaining involves the same elements as a formal table—plates, flatware, glasses, serving pieces and utensils—but the format is looser, with a plate at each place, a napkin and fork on the left and a knife (and soup spoon, if needed) on the right, a water glass, and an all-purpose wineglass or tumbler. Salad can be served on separate plates or piled onto the dinner plate. Dessert plates and flatware are brought out when dessert is served. Napkins can be folded or rolled and bound in simple rings.

FAMILY STYLE Because guests pass food to one another on large platters or in bowls, family-style dinners are convivial and hugely popular. Choose food and drinks that sit well at room temperature. Have guests pass all of the food around at once so no one has to wait long to fill their plate. Wrap very hot dishes in a dish towel or set on a trivet in the middle of the table where everyone can reach.

BUFFETS Arrange food on a sideboard, kitchen counter, picnic table, or even a bookcase, and let guests serve themselves. For a contemporary spin, try a DIY station (see sidebar). Stack plates at the beginning of the buffet line and flatware and napkins at the end so people have a free hand to load their plates; consider wrapping flatware in napkins so it is easier to pick up and carry.

LIGHTING & FLOWERS Place candles and tea lights all around the house to give it a warm glow. On the table, use votives, an array of candlesticks, or a mix of both. Outside, swag the area with patio string lights or paper lanterns; place candles in hurricanes to keep them lit. Instead of flowers, think about bowls of seasonal fruit or vegetables, flowering tree branches in pitchers, herb bouquets in bell jars, or small succulent plants in miniature pots.

OUTDOOR EATING For picnics and barbecues, you may be eating in an area outside with no table. Choose a menu that can be served on one plate and provide napkins that are big enough to spread on laps. Handheld food or food that doesn't require being cut with a knife while balancing a plate on your knees are great choices. Use jelly jars as glasses (you can even transport drinks in them with the tops screwed on). Provide seating wherever possible, and make lounging comfortable with throw pillows, blankets, or even upside-down produce crates.

punches & pitchers

Poking bottles of beer and sodas into a galvanized tub of ice isn't the only way to serve casual beverages. Think about serving punch (page 223) and presenting it in a bowl with a ladle and stemless glasses or cups that match. To keep the punch cold, freeze an ice ring in a Bundt pan (with fruit or herbs in it, if you like) and float it in the punch. Or opt for a big batch of negronis, bloody marys, or other cocktails served in pitchers; large ice cubes will help keep the drinks cold (see page 16).

diy stations

Guests love to get involved in the action, so focus your party on a do-it-yourself station. Set up a panini press (page 48), chili pot (page 49), top-your-own pizza bar (page 142), gazpacho garnishes (page 54), taco bar (page 70), or frittata bar (page 29) with a range of ingredients to choose from, and listen to the laughs and wisecracking about whose version is best. Be sure to have enough plates, bowls, and flatware nearby for people who come back for seconds but have somehow lost track of their gear.

set the stage

Before guests arrive, take a few moments to make sure everything is in its place: gather extra chairs, count wineglasses so you don't end up short, fill water pitchers, ready your playlist, and light the candles.

classic service

Restaurant-style service is well-suited to
formal dinner parties. Food is plated in the
kitchen and delivered to diners in courses,
from salad to dessert. The custom is to
serve from the left and clear from the
right, but don't worry too much about that.

Formal Parties

TABLE SETTINGS

A formal place setting isn't that complicated. The key is to arrange things in order of use. Start with the dinner plate in the center, placing it on top of a charger, if you like. The salad plate goes on top of the dinner plate or on the table to its left. Forks are placed to the immediate left of the dinner plate (the dinner fork closest to the plate and the salad fork farthest away), and the knife and then the spoon to the right, reflecting the hands we use to pick them up. The napkin is placed to the left of the plate or on top of it. Glasses are arranged above the knife with the water glass closest to the plate, then a glass for red wine, and finally a glass for white wine farthest away. The bread plate goes above the forks, with the butter knife on top with the blade pointing in. Dessert plates are brought in with that course and flatware resides over the dinner plate, fork tines to the right and spoon to the left.

SERVING PIECES Present food either restaurant-style (at left), on platters offered at the table by a server, or buffet-style from a sideboard. Take into account which platters, bowls, and serving utensils you need for each dish, as well as salad bowls and bread baskets. Platters of food are not usually placed directly on a formal table.

LINENS Tablecloths, runners, and pressed napkins in neutral tones grace most elegant evenings. However, place mats and high-quality napkins in linen or cotton are lovely, too. Folding the napkin creatively can add extra panache.

SALT & PEPPER SHAKERS Place small individual pairs at each place setting or at least one set on both ends of the table for groups of more than six.

LIGHTING Low, unscented votive candles provide a flattering look and don't block sight lines, but more formal candlesticks and tapers, also unscented, can be used. Be sure to dim overhead lights and wall sconces for ambience.

PLACE CARDS It is up to the hosts to assign seating. Either direct guests as they sit down or use place cards. For very formal occasions, hand-lettered card stock is great, but if you don't have neat handwriting, print place cards in a decorative font. Tie or tuck it into the napkin, place it on the plate, or stand it on a holder that reflects the decor of the table or the theme of the dinner.

COFFEE & TEA Formal dinners often end with coffee and tea, so plan on the necessary cups, saucers, and coffee carafe or teapots. Coffee and dessert can be enjoyed away from the dining table, perhaps in the living room, for a relaxed winding-down with a brandy snifter or dessert wine in hand.

simple elegance

Towering arrangements or massive centerpieces block sight lines and conversation, and the scent can detract from the food. An alternative is to feature one kind of elegant bloom—dahlias, hydrangeas, peonies, tulips, garden roses—in a low-profile arrangement or individual vases along the table, or as single stems at each place setting. Or, place a larger arrangement of the blooms in the center of the table and stagger smaller ones along the table and around the entire room.

Lasting Impressions

Entertaining is about more than serving terrific food and drink. It's also about creating wonderful memories. Plan ahead and add special touches to your event that make it feel out of the ordinary. From party games that encourage guests to mingle to unique desserts and take-home favors, thoughtful extras offer more ways to leave a lasting impression and express your style as a couple.

MAKING MEMORIES

ENGAGE Delight guests by adding an unexpected element to your affair. Hire a wine consultant to guide a tasting, a dance teacher to lead a lesson on the lawn, or a fortune teller to divine everyone's future. Whether you add a teaser to the invite hinting at what's in store, or keep it a surprise, guests will find it unforgettable.

PLAY Simple games can be a great way for friends and family to become acquainted. Choose something that suits your venue—try bocce or horseshoes for an outdoor party, and Liars' Dice or trivia for an indoor one.

CREATE Invite dinner guests to join you in the kitchen. Whether the menu calls for everyone to assemble his or her own pizza, create specialty sushi rolls, or wrap tamales in banana leaves, working together keeps the mood causal and fun.

MEMORABLE FINISHES

BRIGHT ICE POPS Serving pretty homemade popsicles (page 100) on a hot summer day puts a special twist on any outdoor occasion. For a grown-up crowd, add a splash of booze to the mix—not too much or the ice pops won't freeze—such as bourbon with plums or tequila with lime and melon.

SOPHISTICATED S'MORES For an outdoor party, it's hard to beat grown-up s'mores by a fire pit or huddled around the dying embers of a backyard grill or a tabletop hibachi. Indoors, a can of Sterno can provide the flame.

PARTY FAVORS

PORTABLE SYRUPS Preparing big-batch cocktails often means whipping up some simple syrup. Make extra syrup using mint, lavender, hot chile, or other spices to infuse it with flavor before decanting into attractive bottles for take-home gifts.

MASON JAR TREATS Glazed pecans, homemade granola, spicy snack mix, or other easy-to-package homemade treats make terrific favors. Add a bit of rustic twine, hand-write each name on a tag, and set the jars by the door for guests to pick up on their way out.

dress to impress

Simple but thoughtful garnishes
add elegance and colorful flair
to this Pavlova with Summer
Berries (recipe page 163).

CHAPTER ONE

DAYTIME DISHES

Season everything with love

seasonal variety

Frittata is wonderfully adaptable to whatever produce is in season. Try adding shaved zucchini or eggplant in the summertime, diced squash during autumn, and bitter greens in the winter months.

Springtime Frittata

Italian frittatas are traditionally made by combining various ingredients with eggs and cooking the mixture on the stove top. Here, the process is simplified by baking the frittata in the oven. If you like, sauté extra whole asparagus spears and peas for garnish.

SERVES 8–10

2 Tbsp unsalted butter, plus more for greasing

1 lb (500 g) thin asparagus, cut into 1½-inch (4-cm) pieces

2 cups (10 oz/315 g) fresh peas, or 1 package (10 oz/315 g) frozen peas, thawed

2 leeks, including tender green parts, thinly sliced

2 large green onions, chopped

Salt and freshly ground pepper

12 large eggs

⅓ cup (1½ oz/45 g) grated Parmesan cheese

2 Tbsp snipped fresh chives

½ tsp chopped fresh tarragon

½ cup (2 oz/60 g) shredded Swiss cheese

Thinly sliced radishes for garnish (optional)

Preheat the oven to 350°F (180°C). Grease a 9-by-13-inch (23-by-33-cm) or other 2½-quart (2.5-l) baking dish with butter.

In a large skillet over medium heat, melt the butter. Add the asparagus and cook, stirring occasionally, until bright green but not yet tender, 1–2 minutes. Stir in the peas, leeks, and green onions. Season with salt and pepper. Cook, stirring, until the leeks are wilted, 1–2 minutes. Spread the vegetable mixture in the prepared baking dish in one even layer.

In a large bowl, whisk the eggs with ½ teaspoon salt until well blended. Stir in the Parmesan, chives, and tarragon. Pour the egg mixture over the vegetables and top with the Swiss cheese. Bake until the custard is set and lightly browned on top, about 35 minutes. Let cool 5–10 minutes before cutting. If desired, garnish with radish slices.

Cinnamon-Nutmeg Baked French Toast

This delicious spiced toast is a baked spin on traditional French toast. It's quickly assembled and can then be left to bake while you prepare other parts of the meal. For fruity flavor, swap out the maple syrup for blueberry- or cherry-infused syrup (page 250) instead.

SERVES 6

1 cup (8 fl oz/250 ml) half-and-half or whole milk

4 large eggs

2 Tbsp firmly packed light brown sugar

½ tsp ground cinnamon

¼ tsp freshly grated nutmeg

¼ tsp salt

12 slices sweet French bread or other bread

2 Tbsp unsalted butter, melted

Maple syrup, warmed

Preheat the oven to 400°F (200°C). Line two rimmed baking sheets with parchment paper or foil.

In a shallow bowl, whisk together the half-and-half, eggs, brown sugar, cinnamon, nutmeg, and salt. One slice at a time, turn the bread in the egg mixture to coat on both sides, soaking each slice for about 30 seconds. Shake off the excess batter and transfer the soaked bread to the prepared baking sheets.

Bake until the tops are golden, 5–7 minutes. Flip each slice and continue to bake until puffed and golden on the second side, 5–7 minutes longer.

Turn the oven to the broiler setting. Brush the tops of the baked toasts with the melted butter. Place under the broiler until lightly browned, about 1 minute. Serve warm, with the maple syrup.

Pumpkin Muffins with Streusel Topping

The night before you plan to bake the muffins, measure and mix the dry ingredients for the streusel and the batter so the muffins will come together more quickly. Serve for breakfast with protein-packed smoothies or late in the day for a pick-me-up after an afternoon hike.

MAKES 12 MUFFINS

FOR THE STREUSEL

3 Tbsp firmly packed light brown sugar

2 Tbsp all-purpose flour

¼ tsp ground nutmeg

¼ tsp ground cinnamon

¼ cup (1 oz/30 g) pumpkin seeds (pepitas), chopped

1 Tbsp unsalted butter, at room temperature

1½ cups (7½ oz/235 g) all-purpose flour

1 tsp baking soda

½ tsp baking powder

½ tsp salt

½ tsp ground cinnamon

½ tsp ground cloves

½ tsp ground nutmeg

1 cup (8 oz/250 g) canned pumpkin purée

1½ cups (12 oz/375 g) granulated sugar

½ cup (4 fl oz/125 ml) canola oil

2 large eggs, at room temperature, lightly beaten

½ tsp vanilla extract

To make the streusel, in a small bowl, stir together the brown sugar, flour, nutmeg, and cinnamon. Add the seeds and mix well. Add the butter and, using a fork or your fingertips, rub lightly until evenly blended. Set aside.

Preheat the oven to 350°F (180°C). Line a 12-cup muffin pan with paper liners.

To make the muffins, in a bowl, stir together the flour, baking soda, baking powder, salt, cinnamon, cloves, and nutmeg. In a large bowl, combine the pumpkin, granulated sugar, oil, eggs, and vanilla and stir until well mixed. Stir in the flour mixture just until blended.

Divide the batter evenly among the lined muffin cups, and sprinkle evenly with the streusel. Bake until a toothpick inserted into the center of a muffin comes out clean, about 20 minutes. Let the muffins cool in the pan on a wire rack for 5 minutes, then invert the muffins onto the rack, turn upright, and let cool completely. Serve at room temperature.

Caramel-Pecan Sticky Buns

To save time on brunch day, refrigerate the assembled buns the night before, then let rise at room temperature until puffy before baking. Add a sprinkle of flaky sea salt before serving, if you like, for a last-minute infusion of sweet-salty flavor.

MAKES 24 BUNS

FOR THE DOUGH

1 package (2¼ tsp) active dry yeast

¾ cup (6 fl oz/180 ml) whole milk, warmed (110°F/43°C)

¼ cup (2 oz/60 g) granulated sugar

4 large eggs

4½ cups (22½ oz/705 g) all-purpose flour, plus more as needed

1½ tsp salt

6 Tbsp (3 oz/90 g) unsalted butter, at room temperature, cut into chunks, plus more for greasing

FOR THE CARAMEL

6 Tbsp (3 oz/90 g) unsalted butter, melted

1 cup (7 oz/220 g) firmly packed light brown sugar

3 Tbsp dark honey

Pinch of salt

1 cup (4 oz/125 g) coarsely chopped pecans

4 Tbsp (2 oz/60 g) unsalted butter, at room temperature

½ cup (3½ oz/105 g) firmly packed light brown sugar

1 tsp ground cinnamon

variation

Replace the pecans with coarsely chopped almonds and add a handful of dried cherries with the nuts.

To make the dough, in the bowl of a stand mixer, dissolve the yeast in the warm milk and let stand until foamy, about 10 minutes. Add the granulated sugar, eggs, flour, and salt. Attach the dough hook and knead on low speed, adding a little more flour as needed, until the ingredients come together. Add the butter and continue kneading until the dough is smooth and springy, about 7 minutes. Lightly grease a large bowl with butter. Form the dough into a ball, place it in the greased bowl, and cover with plastic wrap. Let it rise at room temperature until doubled, 1½–2 hours.

Butter two 8-inch (20-cm) square baking dishes.

To make the caramel, stir together the melted butter, brown sugar, honey, salt, and pecans. Spread half of the pecan mixture in each pan.

Punch down the dough and dump onto a floured work surface. Cut it in half. Roll each half into a rectangle about 8 by 14 inches (20 by 35 cm). Position them horizontally.

Spread each rectangle with 2 tablespoons of the butter, then half of the brown sugar and half of the cinnamon, leaving a ½-inch (12-mm) border on the side farthest from you. Starting at the side closest to you, roll each rectangle into a log and pinch the seams to seal. Cut each log crosswise into 12 equal slices and arrange, cut side up, in the pans. Cover loosely with plastic wrap and let stand in a warm, draft-free spot until puffy, about 1 hour, then let stand at room temperature for 30–60 minutes.

Position a rack in the middle of the oven and preheat to 350°F (180°C). Bake until golden brown, about 30 minutes. Let cool in the pans on a wire rack for 5 minutes, then invert each pan and unmold the buns onto a plate. When the buns are just cool enough to handle, pull apart and serve warm.

indulgent mornings

Few morning treats are as heavenly as decadent sticky buns. Make these when you want to impress your guests. Add a sprinkle of flaky sea salt just before serving for extra flavor.

MORNING, SUNSHINE *Brunch doesn't have to be a sit-down affair. Instead, set up a buffet with delicious homemade treats, fresh fruit, mimosas, and hot coffee and encourage guests to mingle.*

Zucchini, Basil & Fontina Quichelets

You can turn this recipe into a large quiche by lining a 9-inch (23-cm) tart pan with the dough and partially baking as directed in the recipe. Add the entire amount of filling to the partially baked crust and bake as directed. It might take a few more minutes to finish baking.

SERVES 4

FOR THE PASTRY DOUGH

1¼ cups (6½ oz/200 g) all-purpose flour

¼ tsp salt

7 Tbsp (3½ oz/105 g) cold unsalted butter, cut into cubes

5 Tbsp (3 fl oz/80 ml) ice water, or as needed

2 small zucchini, about 7 oz (220 g) each, trimmed

Salt and freshly ground pepper

3 large eggs

½ cup (4 fl oz/125 ml) heavy cream or half-and-half

1 Tbsp finely chopped fresh basil

½ cup (2 oz/60 g) shredded fontina cheese

To make the dough, in a food processor, combine the flour and salt. Scatter the butter over the top and pulse for a few seconds, or just until the butter is slightly broken up into the flour but is still in visible pieces. Evenly sprinkle the ice water over the flour, then process just until the mixture starts to come together, adding more ice water, 1 teaspoon or so at a time, if the mixture seems too crumbly. Transfer the dough to a large zippered plastic bag and press into a flat disk. Refrigerate for 30 minutes or up to 1 day.

Preheat the oven to 400°F (200°C). Have ready four 4½-inch (11.5-cm) tartlet pans with removable bottoms.

Divide the dough into 4 equal pieces. On a floured work surface, roll each piece into a round about 6 inches (15 cm) in diameter. Line each pan with a round of dough. As you finish each one, put it in the freezer. Line each tart shell with aluminum foil and then fill with pie weights or dried beans. Put the shells on a baking sheet and bake until the dough is set and starting to dry out, about 15 minutes. Remove the foil and weights and continue to bake until the crusts look dry, about 5 minutes. Remove from the oven. Reduce the oven temperature to 375°F (190°C).

Meanwhile, shred the zucchini on the large holes of a box grater-shredder onto paper towels. Spread out the shreds and sprinkle with a little salt. Let stand for about 20 minutes. Using paper towels, blot the zucchini as dry as possible. Divide the shredded zucchini among the tartlet shells. In a bowl, whisk together the eggs, cream, and basil. Season with salt and pepper. Divide the mixture among the pans, pouring it over the zucchini. Sprinkle with the cheese.

Bake until the filling is set and the tops are lightly golden, about 25 minutes. If you want to get the cheese extra bubbly and brown, slide the quichelets in the broiler for 1 minute. Let stand for a few minutes before serving.

Nut & Seed Pancakes with Fresh Berries

These light, fluffy pancakes are ideal for a casual weekend brunch. Be careful not to overmix the batter or the pancakes will be tough. Fry up some bacon and your menu is complete. Warm a pitcher of maple syrup by setting it in a saucepan of water over low heat for a few seconds.

MAKES ABOUT 12 PANCAKES

2 large eggs

2 cups (10 oz/315 g) all-purpose flour

2 Tbsp sugar

2 tsp baking powder

1 tsp baking soda

1 tsp salt

2 cups (16 fl oz/500 ml) buttermilk

4 Tbsp (2 oz/60 g) unsalted butter, melted

1 tsp vanilla extract

2 Tbsp chopped pecans

1 Tbsp sesame seeds

1½ tsp poppy seeds

Canola oil for frying

1 pint (8 oz/250 g) blueberries, blackberries, or a mixture

Maple syrup or Easy Blueberry Syrup (page 250), warmed, for serving

Preheat the oven to 200°F (95°C). In a bowl, beat the eggs until frothy. Add the flour, sugar, baking powder, baking soda, salt, buttermilk, melted butter, and vanilla. Continue to beat just until the mixture is smooth. Add the pecans, sesame seeds, and poppy seeds and beat until combined. Do not overbeat.

Heat a large, heavy frying pan or griddle over high heat until a drop of water flicked on the surface sizzles and immediately evaporates. Lightly oil the pan. Ladle about ⅓ cup (3 fl oz/80 ml) of the batter onto the hot pan for each pancake and cook until bubbles form on the surface, about 2 minutes. Flip the pancakes and cook until the bottoms are golden brown, 1–2 minutes longer. Transfer to a baking sheet and keep warm in the oven. Repeat with the remaining batter.

To serve, spoon berries over each serving of pancakes and drizzle with maple syrup.

Pastry Toasts Four Ways

leeks + pancetta + Gruyère

6 unbaked puff pastry rectangles

2 Tbsp olive oil

2 leeks, halved lengthwise and
cut into 3½-inch (9-cm) lengths

4 slices pancetta, cut into bite-size pieces

½ cup (2 oz/60 g) shredded Gruyère cheese

Preheat the oven to 400°F (200°C). Line a baking sheet with parchment paper. Place the pastry rectangles on the prepared baking sheet. In a sauté pan over medium heat, warm 1 tablespoon of the olive oil. Add the leeks and sauté until softened, about 2 minutes. Transfer to a plate and set aside. In the same pan over medium heat, warm the remaining 1 tablespoon olive oil. Add the pancetta and cook, stirring often, until browned, about 5 minutes. Transfer to paper towels to drain. Sprinkle cheese over the pastry rectangles and arrange the leeks and pancetta on top. Bake until the pastry is puffed, crisp, and golden, about 15 minutes.

smoked bacon + egg

6 puff pastry rectangles, baked according to package directions

8 slices thick-sliced smoked bacon,
cut into ½-inch (12-mm) pieces

2 Tbsp olive oil or unsalted butter

6 large eggs

Salt and freshly ground pepper

In a large frying pan over medium-high heat, fry the bacon until crisp, about 5 minutes. Transfer to paper towels to drain. In a large nonstick frying pan over medium heat, warm 1 tablespoon of the oil. Crack 3 of the eggs into the pan. Sprinkle the eggs with salt and pepper, cover, reduce the heat to medium-low, and cook until the whites begin to set and the yolks thicken, about 2 minutes. Repeat with the remaining 1 tablespoon oil and 3 eggs. Place the prebaked pastry rectangles on warmed plates and top each one with an equal amount of the bacon and a fried egg. Season with salt and pepper.

To make these easy toasts, start with six 6-by-5-inch (13-by-15-cm) pieces of thawed, frozen puff pastry. To give the toasts a rim, cut thin pastry strips and attach them with brushed beaten egg, then brush egg over the rim before baking.

tomatoes + feta + herbs

6 unbaked puff pastry rectangles

1 cup (6 oz/185 g) cherry tomatoes, halved

8 small ripe tomatoes, thinly sliced

6 oz (185 g) feta cheese, sliced

Salt and freshly ground pepper

1 Tbsp fresh oregano leaves

6 sprigs fresh thyme

Preheat the oven to 400°F (200°C). Line a baking sheet with parchment paper. Place the pastry rectangles on the prepared baking sheet and arrange the cherry tomatoes, sliced tomatoes, and feta cheese on top. Season with salt and pepper. Bake until the pastry is puffed, crisp, and golden, about 15 minutes. Sprinkle with the oregano and garnish with the thyme sprigs.

peas + ricotta + mint

1⅓ cups (6½ oz/200 g) fresh English peas
and small lima beans

1 cup (8 oz/250 g) fresh whole-milk ricotta, drained

1 Tbsp finely chopped fresh mint,
plus small fresh mint leaves for garnish

1 tsp minced lemon zest

Salt and freshly ground pepper

6 puff pastry rectangles, baked according to package directions

Bring a small pot of water to a boil over high heat; have ready a bowl of ice water. Add peas and lima beans to boiling water and blanch for 2 minutes. Drain, refresh in ice water, and drain again. Reserve ⅓ cup (1½ oz/45 g) of the pea mixture and set aside. In a food processor, process the remaining peas, ½ cup (4 oz/125 g) of the ricotta, and the chopped mint to make a chunky purée. Stir in the lemon zest and season with salt and pepper. Spread the pea-ricotta mixture evenly over the prebaked pastry rectangles and top with the ricotta, reserved pea mixture, and mint leaves.

Baked Eggs with Spinach & Cream

When it comes to preparing breakfast for friends, nothing is better than a make-ahead, easy morning game plan. Prepare the spinach mixture in advance, fill the ramekins, and refrigerate. Fifteen minutes before mealtime, crack in the egg, add the cream, and bake.

SERVES 4

1 Tbsp unsalted butter, plus more for greasing

1½ lb (750 g) spinach, rinsed but not dried

1 tsp olive oil

3 oz (90 g) prosciutto, chopped

¾ cup (6 fl oz/180 ml) plus 4 tsp heavy cream

Salt and freshly ground pepper

Pinch of freshly grated nutmeg

4 large eggs

4 tsp freshly grated Parmesan cheese

Preheat the oven to 350°F (180°C). Butter four ¾-cup (6–fl oz/180-ml) ramekins.

In a large saucepan over medium heat, melt the butter. A handful at a time, add the spinach, cooking until the first batch wilts before adding another handful. Cook all of the spinach until tender, about 3 minutes. Drain the spinach in a sieve, pressing gently to remove excess liquid. Transfer to a chopping board and coarsely chop.

Heat the oil in the same pan over medium heat. Add the prosciutto and cook, stirring occasionally, until its fat is rendered, about 2 minutes. Add the ¾ cup (6 fl oz/180 ml) cream and the spinach and bring to a boil. Cook, stirring often, until the cream has thickened and reduced to a few tablespoons, about 4 minutes. Season with salt, pepper, and nutmeg. Divide evenly among the prepared ramekins. Break an egg into each ramekin. Season with salt and pepper, and drizzle each with 1 teaspoon cream. Arrange the ramekins on a rimmed baking sheet.

Bake, watching the eggs to avoid overcooking them, until the whites are opaque and the yolks have firm edges and are soft in the center, about 15 minutes. Remove from the oven, sprinkle each serving with 1 teaspoon Parmesan, and serve.

Savory Bread Pudding with Aged Gouda

This rich and cheesy dish is wonderful for breakfast or brunch, especially when paired with sausages or ham. It's ideal for entertaining in the morning because it—like the egg recipe at left—can be assembled the night before baking, so you won't have to wake up extra early to make it.

SERVES 6

½ lb (250 g) coarse country bread

2 Tbsp olive oil

2 cloves garlic, pressed

1 Tbsp unsalted butter, plus more for greasing

1 large shallot, finely chopped

2 Tbsp fresh sage leaves, chopped

4 large eggs

1¾ cups (14 fl oz/430 ml) heavy cream

1 cup (8 fl oz/250 ml) whole milk

½ tsp salt

½ tsp freshly ground pepper

1½ cups (6 oz/185 g) grated aged Gouda cheese

Preheat the oven to 375°F (190°C). Cut the bottom crust and short ends off the bread and discard. Cut the remaining bread into 1-inch (2.5-cm) cubes; you should have about 5 cups (10 oz/315 g). In a large bowl, stir together the olive oil and garlic. Add the bread cubes and toss to coat evenly. Transfer the bread to a large rimmed baking sheet, spreading in an even layer. Bake the cubes, stirring occasionally, until golden and lightly crunchy, about 20 minutes. Set aside.

Meanwhile, in a heavy frying pan over medium heat, melt the butter. Add the shallot and sauté until translucent, about 4 minutes. Add the sage and stir until it turns dark green and fragrant, about 2 minutes. Remove from the heat and let cool.

Generously butter an 8-inch (20-cm) square baking dish. In a large bowl, whisk together the eggs, cream, milk, salt, and pepper. Stir in the shallot-sage mixture and 1 cup (4 oz/125 g) of the cheese. Add the bread cubes and stir to coat. Transfer the mixture to the prepared baking dish and let stand for 20 minutes. (At this point, the dish can be loosely covered with plastic wrap and refrigerated for up to 1 day.)

Sprinkle the top with the remaining ½ cup (2 oz/60 g) cheese. Bake until the bread pudding is set and the top is golden, about 45 minutes. Serve warm or at room temperature.

autumn Treasures

Serve dishes that showcase seasonal produce to take advantage of what's freshest at local farmers' markets and to evoke the changing of the seasons with style.

Baked Apples with Dried Fruit & Honey Glaze

Stuffed with granola, almonds, and dried fruit, these baked apples are a great way to create a warm and comforting morning meal. Drizzle with heavy cream just before serving, if you like.

SERVES 4

1 cup (8 fl oz/250 ml) apple cider

¼ cup (1½ oz/45 g) dried fruit such as currants, cranberries, chopped apricots, or a mix

4 baking apples such as Rome Beauty, Fuji, or Jonagold

1 cup (3 oz/90 g) oat-based granola

¼ cup (1½ oz/45 g) chopped toasted almonds

¼ cup (2 oz/60 g) apple juice concentrate

⅓ cup (4 oz/125 g) honey

In a small saucepan, bring the cider to a boil. Remove from the heat, add the dried fruit, and stir to mix well. Let stand until the fruit has plumped, 30–60 minutes.

Preheat the oven to 350°F (180°C). Using a sharp knife, cut around each stem to remove it with a chunk of apple attached. Set the apple tops aside for serving or discard. Using a melon baller, scoop out each apple core and carve out the flesh to leave a shell ½ inch (12 mm) thick, being careful not to puncture each base. Stand the apples in a baking dish just large enough to hold them upright. Drain the dried fruit in a sieve held over the apples, distributing the cider evenly.

In a medium bowl, stir together the dried fruit, granola, and almonds. Spoon the mixture into the apple cavities, stuffing them high. Cut out four 5-inch (13-cm) square pieces of foil and tent over the stuffing in each apple. Bake until a knife pierces the apple bottoms with only slight resistance but the sides retain their shape, 35–40 minutes. Remove from the oven and lift off the foil. Let the apples cool in the dish for about 20 minutes. Arrange the apples on a platter, spooning any of the stuffing that fell off back in place. Discard the liquid in the dish.

In a saucepan over medium-high heat, bring the apple juice concentrate and honey to a boil. Reduce the heat to medium and simmer until the liquid is syrupy and reduced by about one-third, about 8 minutes. Spoon the hot glaze over the stuffing and apples. Place the apple tops over the filling, if you like, and serve warm or at room temperature.

Brunch Beverages

The key to a fun, casual party is how it gets started. Even if one of you lingers in the kitchen for a few last-minute preparations, the other can welcome guests with a cheery greeting and a cold cocktail. You can't go wrong with any one of these ever-popular drinks.

Cranberry Magic

Ice cubes

½ cup plus 1 Tbsp (4½ fl oz/140 ml) Captain Morgan or other spiced rum

1½ cups (12 fl oz/375 ml) collins mix

1½ cups (12 fl oz/375 ml) cranberry juice

1 lemon, cut into 6 wedges (optional)

Fill a pitcher with ice. Add the spiced rum, collins mix, and cranberry juice and stir to blend. Divide evenly among 6 highball glasses. Garnish each glass with a lemon wedge, if you like, and serve.

SERVES 6

Bellini

3 ripe white peaches, pitted but not peeled, sliced, plus additional slices for garnish (optional)

1 Tbsp fresh lemon juice

1 Tbsp Simple Syrup (page 250)

Crushed ice

2 bottles (24 fl oz/750 ml each) sparkling wine such as cava or Prosecco, chilled

Cherries for garnish (optional)

In a blender, combine the peaches, lemon juice, and simple syrup until smooth.

For guests to self-serve, pour the peach purée into a carafe and nestle the carafe in a large bowl of crushed ice. Place flutes and the bottles of sparkling wine alongside. Instruct guests to fill a flute about one-third full with peach purée, top off with sparkling wine, stir gently to combine, and add garnishes, if using.

SERVES 10–12

Perfect Ramos Fizz

1 cup (8 fl oz/250 ml) gin

3 Tbsp fresh lemon juice

1 Tbsp fresh lime juice

3 Tbsp sugar

4 pasteurized egg whites

3 Tbsp heavy cream

Orange flower water

3 cups (1½ lb/750 g) crushed ice

1⅓ cups (11 fl oz/330 ml) club soda

Freshly grated nutmeg or lemon twists for garnish (optional)

In a blender, combine the gin, lemon juice, lime juice, sugar, egg whites, and cream with a splash of orange flower water and the crushed ice. Blend until frothy, about 1 minute. Divide among 4 highball glasses. Top each one with an equal amount of the club soda. Garnish with nutmeg or lemon, if desired.

SERVES 4

Spicy Bloody Mary

1 lemon, halved

4 cups (32 fl oz/1 l) tomato juice

2 tsp freshly grated horseradish

2 tsp Worcestershire sauce

2 tsp celery salt

1 tsp cayenne pepper

½ tsp paprika

Freshly ground black pepper

2 cups (16 fl oz/500 ml) vodka

Ice cubes

6 ribs celery with leafy tops for garnish

6 long, thin carrot slices for garnish

Squeeze the juice from the lemon halves into a large pitcher. Add the tomato juice, horseradish, steak sauce, celery salt, cayenne, paprika, and a few grinds of black pepper and stir until thoroughly combined. Add the vodka and stir to combine.

Fill 6 tumblers with ice and pour the vodka mixture over the ice, dividing it evenly. Garnish with the celery ribs and carrot slices and serve.

SERVES 6

Micheladas

Coarse sea salt

1 lime wedge for moistening plus 6 lime wedges for garnish

Ice cubes

1½ cups (12 fl oz/375 ml) fresh lime juice

6 dashes Worcestershire sauce

6 dashes hot-pepper sauce

6 bottles (12 fl oz/375 ml each) Mexican beer such as Superior or Bohemia

Pour a layer of salt onto a small plate. Moisten the rim of a tall glass with 1 of the lime wedges and then dip the rim into the salt to coat it evenly. Repeat with 5 more glasses, using the same lime wedge. Place the glasses in the freezer to chill for at least 15 minutes.

When ready to serve, place several ice cubes in each glass. Add ¼ cup (2 fl oz/60 ml) of the lime juice and a dash each of the Worcestershire and hot-pepper sauces to each glass. Pour 1 bottle of beer into each glass, garnish with a lime wedge, and serve.

SERVES 6

Quinoa Bowl with Roasted Vegetables & Goat Cheese

Red quinoa's nutty taste and hefty texture are great with root vegetables. Roasting individual Brussels sprout leaves gives them an irresistible combination of creamy center and caramelized crisp edges.

SERVES 6

3 golden beets

3 Tbsp plus 2 tsp olive oil

Salt and freshly ground pepper

6 oz (180 g) baby carrots, halved lengthwise

1 lb (500 g) large Brussels sprouts, tough outer leaves removed

2 leeks, white and 3 inches (7.5 cm) of green part, thinly sliced

6 cups (39 oz/1.2 kg) cooked red quinoa

6 oz (185 g) fresh goat cheese

¼ cup (⅓ oz/10 g) fresh thyme leaves

⅓ cup (2 oz/60 g) hazelnuts, coarsely chopped

Preheat the oven to 400°F (200°C).

Place the beets in a baking dish just large enough to hold them in a single layer. Drizzle with 1 tablespoon of the oil. Season with salt and pepper, and toss well. Cover the dish with foil and roast until the beets are tender when pierced with a paring knife, 60–75 minutes. Remove the beets from the oven and let cool. Scrape the skin off the beets, then cut them into wedges ½ inch (12 mm) thick and set aside.

In a mixing bowl, drizzle the carrots with 1 tablespoon of the oil and toss to coat. Arrange the carrots in one layer on a baking sheet and roast until the thinner ones are just tender when pierced with the tip of a paring knife, about 20 minutes. Set aside.

Using a paring knife, cut off the base of each brussels sprout and, working from the bottom, peel off individual leaves until the remaining leaves are too tight to remove. In a mixing bowl, toss the leaves with 1 tablespoon of the oil until well coated. Spread them in one layer on a baking sheet. Roast for 20 minutes, or until the edges of the leaves are browned and crisp. Set aside.

In a mixing bowl, combine the leeks with the 2 teaspoons oil and spread them in one layer on a second baking sheet. Roast until the leeks are soft and caramelized in places, about 20 minutes. Transfer the leeks to a medium mixing bowl, add the quinoa, and toss to combine. Set aside.

In a small bowl, mash together the goat cheese, thyme leaves, and a pinch of salt and pepper. Set aside.

Divide the quinoa mixture among 6 wide, shallow bowls. Divide the vegetables among the bowls on top of the quinoa. Sprinkle with hazelnuts. Add a dollop of the goat cheese mixture and serve.

healthy habits

Wholesome grains and fresh produce in
a rainbow of colors look beautiful on the
plate and nourish the body, making it
easy to please all the health-conscious
eaters on your guest list.

The Cubano

Layered with roasted pork, ham, melted cheese, and pickles, this is the most beloved sandwich of the Cuban communities in Tampa and Miami. Here, cilantro is added to update this classic combination, but you can omit it if you want to be authentic.

SERVES 4

4 long Cuban rolls or submarine rolls, split

2 Tbsp unsalted butter, at room temperature

2 Tbsp Dijon mustard

2 Tbsp chopped fresh cilantro (optional)

6 oz (180 g) thinly sliced provolone cheese or Swiss cheese

4 oz (120 g) thinly sliced roasted pork

4 oz (120 g) thinly sliced Black Forest ham

2 dill pickles, thinly sliced

Preheat a panini press. Spread the crust sides of the rolls with the butter, then spread the cut sides with the mustard and sprinkle with cilantro, if using. On the bottom half of each roll, layer one-fourth of the cheese and half of the pork, ham, and pickle slices. Divide the remaining cheese on top. Cover with the top halves of the rolls, mustard sides down, and press gently.

Working with 2 sandwiches at a time, place the panini in the grill, close the top plate, and cook until the bread is golden and toasted, the meats are warmed, and the cheese is melted, 3–5 minutes. Serve hot off the press.

set up a panini bar

DIY cooking stations are at the core of hassle-free entertaining. For your next game night (or other casual event), enjoy the evening as much as your guests by setting out a panini press, along with all the panini fixings, for everyone to make the easy sandwiches for themselves. A pot of chili (see facing page) set simmering alongside makes a nice accompaniment. Set out a ladle on a plate, along with a stack of bowls and some spoons, for simple do-it-yourself service.

Chili con Carne

Long, slow simmering gives this Texas-style chili time to develop a complex, robust flavor and hearty texture. You can garnish the chili with just about anything you like, from sour cream to chopped onions to shredded cheese.

SERVES 4–6

2 lb (1 kg) boneless beef chuck, trimmed and cut into ½-inch (12-mm) cubes

Salt and freshly ground pepper

2 Tbsp canola oil

½ cup (2 oz/60 g) finely chopped mixed chiles such as jalapeño, serrano, and poblano, seeded if desired

1 small red bell pepper, seeded and finely chopped

8 cloves garlic, minced

4 tsp chili powder

1 tsp ground cumin

½ tsp ground coriander

1 can (28 oz/875 g) diced tomatoes with juice

1 tsp dried oregano

2 cups (16 fl oz/500 ml) beef broth or water

Leaves from 12 sprigs fresh cilantro

1 cup (8 oz/250 g) sour cream (optional)

Sprinkle the meat evenly with salt and pepper. In a large, heavy frying pan over medium heat, warm 1 tablespoon of the oil. Working in batches, brown the beef cubes on all sides, about 5 minutes per batch. Transfer the cubes to a large, heavy pot.

In the same frying pan over medium heat, warm the remaining 1 tablespoon oil. Add the chiles, bell pepper, and garlic, and sauté until the vegetables are softened and beginning to turn golden, about 5 minutes. Stir in the chili powder, cumin, and coriander and cook for about 1 minute. Add the tomatoes with their juices and the oregano, season with salt and pepper, and stir well to scrape up any browned bits on the pan bottom.

Add the vegetable mixture to the pot with the beef. Place over medium heat, add the broth, and bring to a gentle boil, stirring occasionally. Reduce the heat to maintain a gentle simmer, cover, and cook until the meat is very tender and the liquid is slightly thickened, about 2½ hours. If the chili is too soupy, uncover the pot for the last 30 minutes to thicken the sauce.

Season with salt and pepper and garnish with cilantro. Serve with sour cream to add at the table, if desired.

Steak Salad with Red Rice, Yellow Tomatoes & Mango

Inspired by flavorful Thai beef salad, this version adds mango and tomatoes to the spicy greens along with grilled steak and the pungent dressing one might expect. Asian red rice makes this salad a striking and complete main dish. The steak can be grilled a day ahead.

SERVES 6

FOR THE MARINADE

¼ cup (2 fl oz/60 ml) soy sauce, preferably low-sodium

2 Tbsp fresh lime juice

1 Tbsp Asian fish sauce

2 Tbsp coconut sugar or turbinado sugar

1 large clove garlic, thinly sliced

½ tsp peeled and grated fresh ginger

¼ tsp freshly ground pepper

¼ cup (2 fl oz/60 ml) peanut oil

1 lb (500 g) flank steak

3 cups (15 oz/470 g) cooked Himalayan red rice or other red rice

2 cups (2 oz/60 g) baby arugula

2 green onions, including tender green tops, thinly sliced

1 cup (1 oz/30 g) watercress sprigs

1 carrot, julienned

½ cup (½ oz/15 g) *each* fresh cilantro, coarsely chopped, and fresh mint leaves

½ pint (3 oz/90 g) yellow grape tomatoes

3 Tbsp fresh lime juice

2 Tbsp Asian fish sauce

1 Tbsp sambal oelek

2 tsp honey

½ tsp salt

3 Tbsp peanut oil

1 cup (6 oz/185 g) diced mango

Chopped peanuts for garnish (optional)

To make the marinade, in a small bowl, whisk together the soy sauce, lime juice, fish sauce, and sugar until the sugar dissolves. Add the garlic, ginger, and pepper. Whisk in the peanut oil. Transfer the marinade to a 4-qt (4-l) resealable plastic bag, add the meat, and seal the bag, pressing out the air. Massage the marinade into the steak. Set the bag on a plate and chill for at least 6 hours and up to 24 hours, turning the bag several times.

Prepare a charcoal or gas grill for direct grilling over medium-high heat, or preheat a stove-top grill pan over medium-high heat.

Remove the steak from the marinade and pat dry with paper towels. Grill, turning the meat every 2 minutes, until grill-marked and an instant-read thermometer inserted into the thickest part registers 120°F (49°C) for medium-rare, 8–10 minutes. Transfer the meat to a cutting board and let it rest for 10 minutes. Cut the steak across the grain on the diagonal into thin slices. (At this point, the steak can be transferred to a plate, covered with plastic wrap, and refrigerated for up to 1 day.)

In a large mixing bowl, combine the steak, rice, arugula, green onions, watercress, carrot, cilantro, mint, and tomatoes. In a small bowl, whisk together the lime juice, fish sauce, sambal oelek, honey, and salt until the salt dissolves. Vigorously whisk in the peanut oil. Pour the dressing over the salad and gently toss until coated.

Divide the salad among 6 dinner plates. Top each salad with the diced mango, garnish with peanuts (if using), and serve.

CHAPTER TWO

ALFRESCO

A little sunshine clears the palate

Simplest Gazpacho

Seek out ripe, flavorful tomatoes for this traditional Spanish soup. For a presentation in the Andalusian style, omit the garnish of oil, cucumber, and bread crumbs and offer small bowls of diced onion, cucumber, red pepper, and toasted bread crumbs for guests to add to their soup at the table. Serve with an ice cube in each bowl, if you like.

SERVES 4–6

1 English cucumber

1 small red bell pepper

8 ripe tomatoes

¼ cup (1 oz/30 g) chopped sweet red onion

1 tsp minced garlic

¼ cup (2 fl oz/60 ml) extra-virgin olive oil, plus more for drizzling

2 Tbsp red wine vinegar, plus more as needed

6 Tbsp (1 oz/30 g) fresh bread crumbs, plus toasted bread crumbs for garnish

Salt

Peel the cucumber, cut lengthwise in half, and remove the seeds with a spoon. Finely dice enough cucumber to measure out 2 tablespoons, set aside, and chop the rest. Remove the core and seeds from the bell pepper. Chop the bell pepper and the tomatoes.

In a food processor or blender, combine the diced cucumber, bell pepper, tomatoes, onion, garlic, olive oil, and vinegar and purée until smooth. Stir in the fresh bread crumbs. Season to taste with salt and vinegar. Cover and refrigerate for at least 2 hours or up to 2 days. Serve cold in chilled bowls, drizzled with olive oil and garnished with the reserved diced cucumber and toasted bread crumbs.

soup starters

For an inspired appetizer at a party, give new meaning to the phrase "cup of soup" by serving individual portions in pretty glassware or handsome mugs, which guests can easily enjoy as they mingle.

easy does it

Sea salt comes in fine-grained or larger crystals and has more flavor than table salt—a little bit goes a long way.

Grilled Shishito Peppers with Sea Salt

Shishito peppers are typically mild, though a hot one sometimes sneaks into a batch. If the weather is cool, you can cook them indoors in a stove-top grill pan. Dust these addictive peppers with flaky sea salt—Maldon or fleur de sel are good choices—and serve on a wood board or metal platter that accents their rustic appeal.

SERVES 6–8

1 lb (500 g) shishito peppers

1–2 lemons, halved

1 Tbsp olive oil

½ tsp flaky sea salt

Prepare a charcoal or gas grill for direct grilling over high heat. Brush and oil the grill grate.

In a bowl, toss the peppers and lemon halves with the oil. Grill the peppers and lemons, turning as needed, until charred on all sides, 3–4 minutes total. Season with salt and serve.

OUTDOOR GATHERINGS

Whether you invite guests to a casual barbecue or to a more formal supper preceded by cocktails, **EATING OUTDOORS** *is always a treat. With a little planning, alfresco events can be especially easy to pull off. Get the party started with savory snacks and drinks and opt for a* **SEASONAL MENU** *and simple place settings. Entertaining as a couple is about sharing time with friends and family—and about making* **WONDERFUL MEMORIES** *in your own backyard.*

Grilled Figs with Prosciutto

When Mission figs come into season in late summer, put this sweet, salty, tangy dish on the menu as a passed hors d'oeuvre before a main course of grilled chicken or pork. Buy ripe but firm figs—they should be plump and give slightly to the touch—and use them right away.

SERVES 6–8

4 ripe figs such as Black Mission

4–6 slices prosciutto

¼ cup (1¼ oz/30 g) fresh goat cheese, at room temperature

Olive oil for brushing

Salt and freshly ground pepper

2 Tbsp balsamic vinegar or balsamic syrup

2 Tbsp honey

Cut the figs in half or quarters lengthwise, depending on their size. Lay the prosciutto slices flat on a work surface. With a sharp knife, cut each slice crosswise into 4 pieces. Spoon 1 teaspoon goat cheese on top of each fig and tightly wrap with a piece of prosciutto. Secure the bundles with toothpicks, if necessary.

Prepare a charcoal or gas grill for direct grilling over medium-high heat. Brush and oil the grill grate.

Lightly brush the fig bundles with olive oil and season with salt and pepper. Grill the bundles directly over the fire, turning often, until grill-marked on all sides, 4–6 minutes total. Move the bundles to indirect heat and drizzle with the balsamic vinegar. Grill, covered, until the figs are cooked through and the cheese melts, about 3 minutes longer.

Transfer the fig bundles to a serving platter, drizzle with the honey, and serve hot.

elegant trays

Passing trays of warm
hors d'oeuvres works
beautifully whether the
occasion is afternoon
alfresco cocktails or an
upscale garden party.
Opt for savory snacks
that can be easily
devoured in a single bite.

Watermelon & Feta Salad

Sweet watermelon, tangy feta, and peppery basil make a surprisingly copacetic flavor combination. A drizzle of olive oil and a squeeze of fresh lemon juice finish the salad perfectly. This starter's cool appeal makes it a splendid introduction to a grilled main course.

SERVES 4–6

1 small seedless watermelon

5 oz (155 g) feta cheese, cubed

½ cup (½ oz/15 g) fresh basil leaves, chopped

¼ cup (2 fl oz/60 ml) extra-virgin olive oil

Juice of 1 lemon

Coarse sea salt and freshly ground pepper

Cut the watermelon into thick slices, then cut off the rind and cut the flesh into cubes. You should have about 3 cups (15 oz/470 g).

Spread the watermelon cubes on a platter. Sprinkle with the feta and basil. Drizzle with the oil and lemon juice, season with salt and pepper, and serve.

Summer Ceviche with Avocado

The best ceviche should always start with a trip to a trusted fish market to select perfectly fresh, firm, translucent fish fillets that smell pleasantly briny. For a stylishly plated first course, omit the tortilla chips and serve the ceviche in martini glasses.

SERVES 6

1 lb (500 g) boneless firm white fish such as snapper or halibut, cut into ½-inch (12-mm) pieces

1⅓ cups (11 fl oz/330 ml) fresh lime juice

¼ cup (1½ oz/45 g) minced white onion

1 red jalapeño chile, minced

1 avocado, peeled, pitted, and diced

¼ cup (⅓ oz/10 g) minced fresh cilantro

2 Tbsp finely chopped fresh mint

Salt and freshly ground pepper

Tortilla chips for serving

In a bowl, stir together the fish, lime juice, onion, and jalapeño. Cover and refrigerate until the fish is opaque throughout, 30–60 minutes.

Using a slotted spoon, transfer the fish, onion, and jalapeño to another bowl, reserving the marinade. To the fish, add the avocado, cilantro, mint, and a pinch each of salt and pepper. Add some of the marinade for more acidity, if needed. Stir gently to mix and serve right away with the tortilla chips.

One secret to stress-free hosting is mastering a handful of dishes that always impress but are quick to prepare. Learn how to whip up this southern Italian classic and you'll turn to it time and again.

Classic Caprese Salad

For an elegant first-course preparation of this Italian favorite, select eight large tomatoes and serve them whole—one for each guest. Cut each tomato crosswise with four evenly spaced slits, without slicing all the way through. Fill each slit with a slice of cheese and a basil leaf. Set each tomato on a small plate, drizzle with the vinaigrette, and serve.

SERVES 8

FOR THE BASIL VINAIGRETTE

2 cups (2 oz/60 g) lightly packed fresh basil leaves

2 small cloves garlic

2 Tbsp red wine vinegar

2 Tbsp balsamic vinegar

1 tsp salt

⅔ cup (5 fl oz/160 ml) extra-virgin olive oil

4 balls fresh mozzarella cheese, about 12 oz (375 g) total weight

2 lb (1 kg) mix of ripe tomatoes, cut into wedges, and red, yellow, and orange cherry tomatoes, halved

Salt and freshly ground pepper

Fresh basil leaves for garnish

To make the vinaigrette, in a food processor, combine the basil, garlic, vinegars, and salt and pulse until the basil is coarsely chopped. With the motor running, drizzle in the olive oil and process just until the vinaigrette is emulsified. Transfer to a small bowl or a glass jar and set aside.

Cut the mozzarella into slices. Arrange the mozzarella and tomatoes on a platter. Drizzle with the basil vinaigrette (you may not need all of it), season with salt and pepper, garnish with basil leaves, and serve.

Shaved Zucchini Salad with Lemon & Mint

You can use either a mandoline or a vegetable peeler to shave the zucchini. If you opt for the vegetable peeler, look for one that is serrated and designed for soft vegetables. Seek out a top-notch fruity extra-virgin olive oil to infuse this dish with a rich, distinctive flavor.

SERVES 4–6

4 zucchini, about 2 lb (1 kg) total weight

¼ cup (2 fl oz/60 ml) extra-virgin olive oil

1 tsp finely grated lemon zest

Salt and freshly ground pepper

¼ cup (⅓ oz/10 g) torn fresh mint leaves

Crumbled Parmesan cheese for garnish (optional)

Borage flowers for garnish (optional)

Trim the ends of the zucchini but do not peel. Using a vegetable peeler or a mandoline, shave the zucchini lengthwise into long, paper-thin strips, letting the strips fall into a bowl. (If you are unable to shave the seedy cores, discard them or reserve for another use.)

In a small bowl, whisk together the olive oil and lemon zest. Drizzle over the zucchini and season with ¼ teaspoon each salt and pepper. Add the mint and toss gently. Taste and adjust the seasoning. Divide the salad among individual plates, garnish with the Parmesan and/or borage flowers (if using), and serve.

summer beauties

Use edible flowers like borage and nasturtium, or fragrant herbs like mint, thyme, and basil, to add a beautiful final touch to any recipe.

appetizing starters

Family-style dining—bringing food to the table on large platters for sharing—is perfect for casual occasions. Traditional favorites from around the world offer plenty of inspiration for entertaining, with delicious options such as a selection of Greek mezes, Italian antipasti, French charcuterie, or this easy, colorful preparation from Spain.

Grilled Vegetables with Romesco Sauce

Peppers, eggplant, and tomatoes ripen together at the height of the summer season and are excellent choices for grilling. Romesco sauce, a versatile Spanish condiment, goes well with almost any grilled food.

SERVES 4–8

FOR THE ROMESCO SAUCE

½ cup (3 oz/90 g) roasted red peppers

⅓ cup (2 oz/60 g) raw almonds

1 slice sourdough bread, crust removed

2 cloves garlic

2 Tbsp red wine vinegar

½ tsp red pepper flakes

¼ cup (2 fl oz/60 ml) extra-virgin olive oil

1 red onion, thickly sliced

1 large red bell pepper, stemmed, seeded, and cut into thick strips

3 mini bell peppers, halved

1 *each* Japanese eggplant and zucchini, cut lengthwise into slices about ½ inch (12 mm) thick

2 tomatoes, halved crosswise

Salt and freshly ground black pepper

Olive oil for drizzling

Balsamic vinegar for drizzling (optional)

Crostini (page 248), optional

To make the sauce, in a blender or food processor, combine the roasted peppers, almonds, bread, garlic, vinegar, and red pepper flakes and process until fairly smooth. With the machine running, slowly pour in the olive oil and process until the sauce emulsifies. (The sauce can be made 1 day in advance and refrigerated. Bring to room temperature before using.)

Prepare a charcoal or gas grill for direct grilling over medium heat. Brush and oil the grill grate.

Arrange all of the vegetables on a large rimmed baking sheet. Sprinkle with salt and pepper and drizzle with some olive oil. Toss to coat lightly.

Place the onion slices and peppers, skin side down, over the hottest part of the fire. Grill the onions, turning once, until slightly charred but still holding their shape, 4–5 minutes on each side. Transfer to a platter. Grill the peppers until the skins are blackened, 8–10 minutes.

Grill the eggplant and zucchini, turning once, until lightly charred and tender when pierced with a knife, about 8 minutes total. Grill the tomatoes, turning once, until charred on all sides and starting to soften, 5–8 minutes total. Transfer to a platter.

Drizzle the vegetables with more olive oil and some balsamic vinegar, if desired. Season to taste with salt and pepper. Serve with the romesco on the side and, if using, crostini.

Carne Asada Tacos

These classic steak tacos—with authentic seasonings and meat—taste similar to the type found at many top-notch taco trucks.

SERVES 6

4 tsp ground cumin

2 tsp sugar

1 tsp ground coriander

2 lb (1 kg) flank or skirt steak

1 lime, halved, plus lime wedges for serving

4 cloves garlic, coarsely chopped

2 Tbsp chopped fresh cilantro

Salt and freshly ground pepper

12 soft corn or flour tortillas, warmed

Smoky Tomato Salsa (page 73)

2 avocados, thinly sliced

Prepare a charcoal or gas grill for direct grilling over high heat. Brush and oil the grill grate. In a small bowl, mix the cumin, sugar, and coriander. Sprinkle the steak evenly on both sides with the spice mixture, then squeeze 1 lime half over each side. Rub the garlic and cilantro into both sides of the steak, then season both sides generously with salt and pepper. Place on the grill rack and cook, turning once, for 4 minutes per side for medium-rare or 12 minutes per side for medium. Transfer the steak to a cutting board and let rest for 5 minutes. Thinly slice the steak across the grain. To assemble each taco, place a few slices of steak onto a tortilla, add a spoonful of the salsa, and 1 or 2 slices of avocado. Squeeze lime over the top and serve.

Fish Tacos

Fish tacos couldn't be easier to make. Use the freshest fish you can find, substituting cod for the tilapia if necessary.

SERVES 6

¼ tsp *each* ground cumin and dried oregano

½ tsp salt

1 lb (500 g) tilapia or other mild white-fish fillets, pin bones removed

1 Tbsp olive oil

Juice of 1 lime

12 corn tortillas, warmed

2 cups (6 oz/185 g) green cabbage, finely shredded

Grilled Pineapple Salsa (page 72)

⅓ cup (3 oz/90 g) sour cream

2 Tbsp coarsely chopped fresh cilantro

Prepare a charcoal or gas grill for direct grilling over medium-high heat. Brush and oil the grill grate. In a small bowl, mix the cumin, oregano, and salt. Cut fish fillets lengthwise into halves and sprinkle with the spice mixture. Drizzle with the oil and lime juice. Place on the grill rack and cook, turning once, until golden, 3 minutes on the first side, 1–2 minutes on the second side. Transfer the fish to a plate and cut into bite-size pieces. To assemble each taco, spoon some fish onto each tortilla, along with some of the cabbage, a spoonful of salsa, and a dollop of sour cream. Sprinkle with cilantro and serve.

Carnitas Tacos

In Mexico, carnitas *refers to "little meats," or small shreds of well-browned pork. Pork shoulder is an especially tender slow-cooked cut.*

SERVES 8–10

Salt and freshly ground pepper

1 boneless pork shoulder roast, 3–4 lb (1.5–2 kg)

¼ cup (2 fl oz/60 ml) olive oil

1 white onion, finely chopped, plus more for serving

2 cloves garlic, minced

1 bottle (12 fl oz/375 ml) Mexican lager-style beer

Grated zest and juice of 1 large orange and 1 lime

1 Tbsp dried oregano

16–20 flour tortillas, warmed

Mango-Habanero Salsa (page 72) or Grilled Tomatillo Salsa (page 73)

Preheat the oven to 350°F (180°C). In a small bowl, mix 2 teaspoons salt and 1 teaspoon pepper and season the pork. In a large, heavy pot over medium-high heat, warm the oil. Add the pork and sear, turning frequently, until browned on all sides, about 10 minutes. Transfer to a plate. Pour off all but a thin layer of fat from the pot and return to medium-high heat. Add the onion and garlic and sauté until beginning to soften, 1–2 minutes. Add the beer and stir to scrape up any browned bits on the pot bottom. Return the pork and any juices to the pot. Add the orange and lime zests and juices and the oregano. Cover and cook over low heat until the pork is very tender, about 2½ hours. Transfer the pork to a cutting board and cover loosely with foil. Skim the fat from the surface of the cooking liquid. Cut and shred the pork into bite-size pieces, place on a platter, and moisten with the cooking juices. To assemble each taco, spoon some pork onto each tortilla and top with the salsa.

Chicken Tacos

For a tasty taco combo, add a sprinkling of spicy cheese and some shredded lettuce to the chicken and tomatilla salsa.

SERVES 6

¾ tsp ground cumin

¾ tsp dried oregano

Salt

2¼ lb (1.1 kg) boneless, skinless chicken breast halves

3 Tbsp olive oil

Juice of 3 limes

Grilled Tomatillo Salsa (page 73)

12 soft corn or flour tortillas, warmed

Prepare a charcoal or gas grill for direct grilling over medium-high heat. Brush and oil the grill grate. In a small bowl, mix the cumin, oregano, and ½ teaspoon salt. Sprinkle the mixture over all sides of the chicken, then drizzle with the olive oil and lime juice. Place on the grill rack and cook, turning once, until opaque throughout, 3–4 minutes per side. Transfer the chicken to a cutting board and let rest for 5 minutes. Thinly slice the chicken across the grain. To assemble each taco, place a few slices of the chicken and some of the salsa on each tortilla and serve.

Salsa Four Ways

Whether you're serving tacos (pages 70–71), grilled fish or meat, or just plain scrambled eggs, a good freshly made salsa adds bright flavor to any dish.

Mango-Habanero Salsa

2 ripe mangoes, peeled and diced

¼ cup (1½ oz/45 g) finely chopped red onion

2 green onions, including tender green tops, thinly sliced

½ habanero chile, finely chopped

1 Tbsp fresh orange juice

1 Tbsp fresh lime juice

1 tsp grated orange zest

Salt and freshly ground pepper

In a bowl, combine the mangoes, red and green onions, habanero, orange and lime juices, and orange zest and stir well, mashing some of the fruit on the side of the bowl with the spoon. Season with salt and pepper, then let stand at room temperature for 30 minutes before serving to allow the flavors to blend.

Guacamole

¼ cup (1 oz/30 g) finely chopped white onion

1 jalapeño chile, seeded and finely chopped

¼ cup (⅓ oz/10 g) chopped fresh cilantro, plus more for garnish

Salt

2 ripe avocados, halved and pitted

Fresh lime juice

Use a mortar and pestle or a bowl and fork to mash the onion, chile, chopped cilantro, and a pinch of salt to form a coarse paste. Scoop out the flesh of the avocados with a spoon, add to the mixture, and mash until well incorporated. Season to taste with salt and lime juice. Garnish with cilantro.

Grilled Pineapple Salsa

½ fresh pineapple, peeled, cored, and sliced

1 red onion, thickly sliced

1 jalapeño chile, halved and seeded

Olive oil for brushing

½ avocado, peeled and diced

1 Tbsp finely chopped fresh mint

Juice of 1 lime

Salt

Lightly brush the pineapple, onion, and jalapeño with olive oil. Grill until well-marked and heated through. Transfer to a cutting board. Chop the pineapple and onion. Mince the chile. Mix all in a bowl with the avocado, mint, lime juice, and salt.

Grilled Tomatillo Salsa

7 large tomatillos, papery husks removed

1 jalapeño chile, halved lengthwise and seeded

¼ cup (2 fl oz/60 ml) fresh lime juice

1 Tbsp olive oil

½ cup (¾ oz/20 g) chopped fresh cilantro

Salt

Grill the tomatillos and chile until charred. Place in a blender, add the lime juice and olive oil, and pulse until combined but still chunky. Pour into a bowl, stir in the cilantro, and season with salt.

Smoky Tomato Salsa

3 large ripe tomatoes, thickly sliced

1 small red onion, thickly sliced

1 jalapeño chile, halved lengthwise and seeded

Olive oil for brushing

Juice of 2 limes

¼ cup (⅓ oz/10 g) finely chopped fresh cilantro

Salt and freshly ground pepper

Lightly brush the tomatoes, onion, and jalapeño with oil. Grill, turning once, until lightly charred. Transfer to a cutting board, chop coarsely, and place in a bowl. Stir in the lime juice and cilantro. Purée half of the mixture in a food processor and return to the bowl. Season to taste with salt and pepper and mix well.

Corn on the Cob with Lime Butter

Mexican-style hot corn on the cob slathered with butter is one of summer's great eating pleasures. Make the butter a day or two in advance, so that cooking the corn is all that's left to do before serving. Be sure to pull the corn from the fire while the kernels still have snap.

SERVES 6

FOR THE CILANTRO-LIME BUTTER

½ cup (4 oz/125 g) unsalted butter, at room temperature

2 Tbsp minced fresh cilantro

Finely grated zest of 1 lime

1 Tbsp fresh lime juice

6 ears corn

Ancho chile powder or other chile powder

Salt

To make the cilantro-lime butter, in a small bowl, mash together the butter, cilantro, lime zest, and lime juice. Cover and set aside. (The butter can be made ahead and stored in an airtight container in the refrigerator for up to 2 days. Bring to room temperature before serving.)

Remove the husks and silks from the ears of corn. To boil the corn, bring a large pot of water to a boil over high heat. Add the corn and cook until the kernels are tender-crisp, about 5 minutes. Drain well. To grill the corn, prepare a charcoal or gas grill for direct grilling over medium heat. Brush and oil the grill grate. Place the corn on the grill rack directly over the fire and cook, turning every couple of minutes, until tender and evenly but lightly charred, 5–8 minutes.

Transfer the corn to a serving platter. Serve the corn piping hot, with the cilantro-lime butter, chile powder, and salt on the side for guests to add as they like.

more butter flavors

If you want to give your guests more tasty options, whip up another one—or two—of these flavorful butters for dressing the hot corn at the table. For each butter, begin with ½ cup (4 oz/125 g) softened unsalted butter, then work in the seasonings.

SOUTHERN-STYLE SORGHUM BUTTER Blend in juice of ½ lemon, 1 tablespoon sweet sorghum syrup or molasses, and salt.

ROASTED GARLIC BUTTER Blend in 1½ teaspoons roasted garlic paste, ¼ teaspoon salt, and ⅛ teaspoon ground black pepper.

CHILE BUTTER Blend in 1 teaspoon chile powder, ½ teaspoon ground cumin, and ⅛ teaspoon cayenne pepper.

Jicama Slaw with Chile-Lime Dressing

Fresh jicama is a favorite of roadside stands in Mexico, where it is commonly served dressed with a squeeze of lime and a sprinkle of chile powder. This interpretation of the popular combo is a bit more refined, mixing shredded jicama and carrot with a creamy, spicy lime dressing.

SERVES 8–10

1½ lb (750 g) jicama

¾ lb (375 g) carrots

1 cup (1 oz/30 g) loosely packed fresh cilantro leaves

1 jalapeño chile

¼ cup (2 fl oz/60 ml) fresh lime juice

¼ cup (2 oz/60 g) sour cream

¼ cup (2 fl oz/60 ml) mayonnaise

1 tsp salt

½ tsp chili powder

Using a vegetable peeler, peel the jicama and the carrots, then coarsely shred them using the largest holes of a box grater. (Alternatively, use a spiralizer or mandoline to cut the vegetables into long julienne strips.) You should have about 4 cups firmly packed shredded jicama and 2 cups shredded carrot.

Finely chop the cilantro leaves. Halve, seed, and mince the jalapeño.

In a large glass or ceramic bowl, whisk together the lime juice, sour cream, mayonnaise, salt, chili powder, cilantro, and jalapeño. Add the jicama and carrot and toss to mix. Cover and refrigerate for at least 1 hour or up to 3 hours to allow the flavors to blend.

Remove the slaw from the refrigerator just before serving. Toss again to distribute the dressing and serve.

Chicken, Shellfish & Sausage Paella

A grill is perfect for cooking paella: you sear the chicken and chorizo, sauté the vegetables, add the remaining ingredients, and the paella cooks while you open a Spanish wine or mix up some sangria (page 88). Have all of the ingredients ready to use before your guests arrive.

SERVES 6

¼ tsp saffron threads

6 bone-in, skin-on chicken thighs

Salt and freshly ground pepper

1 Spanish dry-cured chorizo sausage

¼ cup (2 fl oz/60 ml) olive oil

3 tomatoes, finely chopped

1 yellow onion, finely chopped

4 cloves garlic, minced

1 Tbsp chopped fresh thyme leaves

½ tsp smoked paprika

1 cup (7 oz/220 g) short-grain paella rice such as Bomba

4 cups (32 fl oz/1 l) chicken broth, preferably low-sodium

16 mussels, manila clams, or a combination, scrubbed

1 jar (7 oz/220 g) roasted red peppers, drained and cut into strips

½ cup (2½ oz/75 g) fresh or frozen English peas

1 lb (500 g) shrimp, unpeeled

Chopped fresh flat-leaf parsley leaves

1 lemon, cut into 6 wedges

authentic paella

The pan traditionally used to make paella—a *paellera*—gives the dish its name. The investment in authenticity pays off in flavor: the pan's shallow, wide, and slightly sloping sides ensure that the rice cooks evenly and in one layer. A large, stainless steel frying pan also works well.

In a small bowl, add the saffron threads to ¼ cup (2 fl oz/60 ml) hot water and set aside. Prepare a charcoal or gas grill for direct grilling over high heat. Brush and oil the grill grate.

Season the chicken with salt and pepper. Slice the chorizo. Place a 15-inch (38-cm) paella pan on the grill directly over the fire, let it heat for a few minutes, and add the oil. When the oil is hot, add the chicken thighs, skin side down, and sear, turning once, until nicely browned on both sides, about 5 minutes per side. Add the chorizo and cook, turning often, until browned, about 5 minutes. Transfer the chicken and chorizo to a platter.

Add the tomatoes, onion, garlic, thyme, and paprika to the oil remaining in the pan and cook, stirring often, until softened, about 5 minutes. Season with salt and pepper. Stir in the rice and cook, stirring, until lightly toasted, 2–3 minutes. Pour in 2 cups (16 fl oz/500 ml) of the broth and bring to a boil. Cover the grill and cook for about 10 minutes without stirring.

Arrange the reserved chicken and chorizo evenly over the rice, then nestle the chicken into the rice. Add 1 cup (8 fl oz/250 ml) of the broth, re-cover the grill, and cook for another 20 minutes without stirring. Add the mussels, hinge side down, distributing them evenly. Top the rice evenly with the pepper strips, peas, and shrimp. If the rice looks dry, add as much of the remaining broth as needed to moisten. Re-cover and cook until the shrimp are opaque and the mussels have opened, about 10 minutes. Discard any mussels that did not open.

Remove the paella from the grill, sprinkle with the parsley, and serve with the lemon wedges.

Spicy Shrimp Kebabs with Chipotle Sauce

Grilling shrimp in the shell is the best way to ensure they retain their tasty juices during cooking. The chipotle sauce and potent cumin rub impart plenty of extra flavor to the shellfish. Have a cooler filled with ice-cold beer and soda to temper the intensity of both the seasoning and the smoke.

SERVES 4–6

FOR THE CHIPOTLE SAUCE

1 chipotle chile in adobo sauce

½ cup (4 oz/125 g) sour cream

½ cup (4 fl oz/125 ml) mayonnaise

1 tsp fresh lime juice

2 Tbsp chopped fresh cilantro

Salt and freshly ground pepper

48 large unpeeled shrimp, about 2 lb (1 kg) total weight

2 Tbsp canola oil, plus more for oiling

2 Tbsp ground cumin

½ tsp smoked paprika

½ tsp firmly packed light brown sugar

¼ tsp cayenne pepper

To make the chipotle sauce, finely chop the chile. In a bowl, whisk together the chile, sour cream, mayonnaise, and lime juice. Stir in the cilantro and season with salt and pepper. Cover and refrigerate until ready to serve. (At this point, the sauce can be stored in an airtight container in the refrigerator up to 4 days.)

Place the shrimp and oil in a large bowl and toss to coat evenly. In a small bowl, stir together the cumin, paprika, brown sugar, and cayenne. Sprinkle the mixture over the shrimp and toss again to coat evenly.

Prepare a charcoal or gas grill for direct grilling over high heat. Brush and oil the grill grate. To make the shrimp easier to turn on the grill, thread them onto skewers. (If using wood skewers, soak them in water for at least 30 minutes before using.) Hold 2 skewers parallel about 1 inch (2.5 cm) apart and thread the shrimp onto both skewers, once near the tail and once near the head. Place the shrimp on the grill directly over the fire and cook for 3 minutes. Turn and cook until the shrimp turn creamy white, 2–3 minutes longer, pulling the shrimp off the grill as soon as they turn opaque.

Let everyone peel their own shrimp. Serve with the chipotle sauce for dipping and plenty of napkins.

Plank-Grilled Salmon with Mustard Sauce

Salmon grilled on a cedar plank, a Pacific Northwest tradition, picks up flavor from both the plank and the smoky fire. Here, the salmon is served with an East Coast deli–inspired honey mustard and dill sauce. Accompany this elegant main course with a full-bodied white or fruity red wine.

SERVES 6

Beer for soaking (optional)

½ cup (4 oz/125 g) unsalted butter

¼ cup (2 fl oz/60 ml) fresh lemon juice

2 Tbsp chopped fresh flat-leaf parsley

1 tsp soy sauce or tamari, preferably low-sodium

Olive oil for brushing

Salt

1 large center-cut salmon fillet or 6 small fillets, 2 lb (1 kg) total weight and about 1 inch (2.5 cm) thick, skin on and pin bones removed

½ cup (4 oz/125 g) honey mustard

¼ cup (⅓ oz/10 g) chopped fresh dill

Soak 1 large or 3 small untreated cedar planks in beer or water to cover for at least 1 hour. (Make sure the large plank is big enough to hold the large fillet or each small plank is large enough to hold 2 small fillets.)

Prepare a charcoal or gas grill for direct grilling over high heat. Brush and oil the grill grate.

In a small saucepan over medium heat, melt the butter. Whisk in the lemon juice, parsley, and soy sauce. Remove from the heat and keep warm.

Remove the plank from the beer or water. Brush one side generously with olive oil and sprinkle with salt. Place the plank, oil side up, on the grill directly over the fire, cover the grill, and heat until it begins to crackle and even smoke a bit, about 5 minutes. Have a spray bottle filled with water handy to extinguish any flames (but be careful—the steam created from the water can cause burns).

Uncover the grill and place the salmon fillet on the plank. Brush generously with the butter mixture. Re-cover and cook, without turning, until the fish flakes when prodded gently with a fork, 10–12 minutes for medium, which is perfect for salmon. Check the plank frequently to make sure it doesn't catch on fire.

Using heavy-duty pot holders, transfer the plank to a heatproof work surface. Using a spatula, transfer the salmon to a warmed platter. In a small bowl, stir together the mustard and dill. Serve the salmon with the mustard-dill sauce on the side.

fresh extras

If you're sometimes too busy to grind spices or make salsa from
scratch, source what you need from a top-notch local market.
Occasional shortcuts will make you a more relaxed host.

Cumin-Crusted Halibut with Grilled Tomatillo Salsa

Here, cumin, smoked paprika, and other bold spices in the rub join a chunky tomatillo salsa to deliver an explosion of flavors to mild-tasting halibut. Grilling tomatillos mellows their natural acidity. Omit the grilling and serve them raw if you prefer their innate tang.

SERVES 6

FOR THE CUMIN CRUST RUB

¼ cup (1 oz/30 g) ground cumin

1 tsp smoked paprika

1 tsp firmly packed light brown sugar

¼ tsp ground coriander

¼ tsp cayenne pepper

Freshly ground black pepper

6 halibut fillets, each about 6 oz (180 g) and 1 inch (2.5 cm) thick

1½ Tbsp mayonnaise

Cilantro sprigs for garnish (optional)

Grilled Tomatillo Salsa (page 73) for serving

Prepare a charcoal or gas grill for direct grilling over high heat. Brush and oil the grill grate.

To make the rub, in a small, dry frying pan over low heat, toast the cumin, stirring often, until aromatic, about 30 seconds. Pour onto a plate and let cool. In an airtight container, combine the cumin, paprika, brown sugar, coriander, cayenne, and ½ teaspoon black pepper. Cover and shake vigorously to mix.

Brush the fish on both sides with the mayonnaise, coating it evenly. Sprinkle each fillet all over with the rub, using about ½ tablespoon per fillet. (Reserve the remaining rub for other uses. Store it in the covered container in a cool, dark place for up to 1 month.)

Place the fish on the grill rack directly over the fire and cook, turning once, until just opaque throughout and the fish flakes easily when prodded gently with a fork, about 4 minutes per side.

Transfer the fillets to a platter or individual plates, and garnish with cilantro sprigs, if using. Serve with the tomatillo salsa.

Marinated Steak with Corn, Arugula & Tomato Salad

Ground sumac—a deep red spice available at Middle Eastern markets—along with cumin and feta give this flavorful grilled steak exotic zip, and the chunky, fresh salad makes for a lovely garnish and bright counterpoint to the beef. This vibrant dish is a real crowd-pleaser. Mound it on a big platter and let guests serve themselves.

SERVES 4

2 Tbsp extra-virgin olive oil

2 Tbsp fresh lemon juice

2 cloves garlic, pressed

2 tsp ground cumin

2 tsp ground sumac

1 lb (500 g) flank steak

Salt and freshly ground pepper

1 ear corn, preferably yellow, husk and silks removed

2 cups (2 oz/60 g) arugula leaves

2 cups (¾ lb/375 g) cherry tomatoes, halved

2 green onions, thinly sliced

2 Tbsp chopped fresh flat-leaf parsley

½ cup (2 oz/60 g) crumbled feta cheese

In a small bowl, whisk together the olive oil, lemon juice, garlic, cumin, and sumac. Place the steak on a plate. Spoon half of the dressing over both sides of the steak, then sprinkle both sides with salt and pepper. Let stand at room temperature for 15 minutes or cover and refrigerate overnight.

Prepare a charcoal or gas grill for direct grilling over medium-high heat. Brush and oil the grill grate. Place the steak over the hottest part of the fire and cook, turning once, until seared on both sides and medium-rare inside, about 8 minutes total. Transfer the steak to a carving board and let rest for at least 5 minutes.

Meanwhile, place the corn on the grill and cook, turning every couple of minutes, until it is lightly charred all the way around and the kernels are tender, 5–7 minutes. Remove from the heat and set aside until cool enough to handle. Stand the corn, flat end down, on a cutting board and cut the kernels from the cobs.

In a bowl, combine the corn kernels, arugula, tomatoes, green onions, parsley, and feta. Drizzle with the remaining dressing, season with salt and pepper, and toss to mix well. Slice the steak, arrange the slices on a platter, place the arugula salad alongside, and serve.

Coconut Rice with Gingery Green Onions

Once this fragrant rice is simmering over low heat, you can turn your attention fully to finishing up other dishes you're preparing. That makes this recipe an especially good choice for menus with dishes that require last-minute attention. If you're including the shaved coconut, purchase it pre-toasted or toast it a day or two in advance.

SERVES 6

1 Tbsp canola oil

2 green onions (including tender green tops), minced

1 tsp peeled and grated fresh ginger

2 cups (14 oz/440 g) jasmine rice, rinsed

1 cup (8 fl oz/250 ml) coconut milk

Salt

½ cup (2 oz/60 g) shaved coconut, toasted (optional)

In a large saucepan over medium-high heat, warm the canola oil. Add the green onions and ginger and sauté until fragrant, about 30 seconds. Add the rice and stir to mix well. Add 2 cups (16 fl oz/500 ml) water, the coconut milk, and 1 teaspoon salt and bring to a boil. Reduce the heat to low, cover, and simmer for 20 minutes. Remove from the heat and let the rice stand, covered, until tender, about 10 minutes longer. Fluff the rice with a fork, stir in the toasted coconut, if using, and serve.

Orzo Salad with Radicchio & Arugula

Serve this salad with grilled Italian sausages and your favorite gelato for a casual backyard lunch or dinner. Or pack it into a picnic basket along with Harissa-Rubbed Chicken (page 93) or Barbecued Baby Back Ribs (page 92) and some fruit-filled hand pies (page 104) and head for the mountains or the beach.

SERVES 6

1½ cups (10½ oz/330 g) orzo

¼ cup (2 fl oz/60 ml) extra-virgin olive oil

2 cloves garlic, pressed

¼ cup (2 fl oz/60 ml) balsamic vinegar

½ cup (1½ oz/45 g) thinly sliced green onions

1 cup (1 oz/30 g) baby arugula leaves

1 cup (3 oz/90 g) thinly sliced radicchio or other red chicory

½ cup (2 oz/60 g) freshly grated Parmesan cheese

½ cup (2½ oz/75 g) toasted pine nuts

¼ cup (¼ oz/7 g) fresh flat-leaf parsley leaves, chopped

Salt and freshly ground pepper

Bring a pot of water to a rapid boil and season generously with salt. Add the orzo, stir well, and cook, stirring occasionally, until al dente, 7–9 minutes or according to package directions. Drain (do not rinse) the orzo and transfer to a large bowl. Immediately stir in the olive oil and garlic and let stand until cool. Stir in the vinegar, then the green onions, arugula, radicchio, Parmesan, pine nuts, and parsley, distributing the ingredients evenly. Season to taste with salt and pepper and serve.

slather it on

An easy way to dress up butter is to add fresh garlic, as in this recipe, or to mix in fragrant herbs. It's the kind of homemade touch that your guests will remember when they think back on the meal.

Grilled T-Bone Steak with Grilled Scallions & Garlic Butter

Here is an easy main course for a relaxed summer evening with friends. Thick T-bone steaks turn out especially succulent and flavorful when cooked on an outdoor grill. The garlic butter, which can be made a few days in advance, is an easy way to add a special finish.

SERVES 4

FOR THE GARLIC BUTTER

½ cup (4 oz/125 g) salted butter, at room temperature

1 Tbsp minced fresh thyme

4 cloves garlic, minced

1–2 dashes Worcestershire sauce

1–2 dashes Tabasco or other hot-pepper sauce

4 T-bone steaks, 10 oz (315 g) each

2 Tbsp olive oil, plus more for brushing

Leaves from 3 sprigs fresh thyme

Kosher salt and freshly ground pepper

12 green onions, trimmed but left whole

2 Tbsp chopped fresh flat-leaf parsley

To make the garlic butter, in a small bowl, combine the butter, thyme, garlic, Worcestershire, and Tabasco. Using a fork, stir and mash until evenly blended. Place a piece of waxed paper on a work surface and spoon the butter mixture on top. Wrap the waxed paper over the butter, roll into a log, and refrigerate until ready to use.

Rub the steaks with the olive oil and thyme and season with 1½ teaspoons salt and a few grinds of pepper.

Prepare a charcoal or gas grill for direct grilling over medium-high heat. Brush and oil the grill grate.

Brush the green onions lightly with olive oil and sprinkle with salt. Place the steaks on the grill directly over the fire and cook, turning once, until medium-rare, 5–6 minutes per side. Add the green onions to the grill after you turn the steaks and cook, turning to brown evenly, until charred and tender, 6–8 minutes total. When the steaks are ready, remove them from the grill and place them on a platter with the green onions.

Place a pat or two of the garlic butter on each steak along with a sprinkling of parsley. Let rest for 3–5 minutes before serving.

Plum & Apricot Sangria

3 plums, halved, pitted, and cut into thin wedges

3 apricots, halved, pitted, and cut into thin wedges

1½ cups (12 fl oz/375 ml) apricot nectar

¼ cup (2 fl oz/60 ml) orange liqueur

1 bottle (750 ml) dry white wine

Ice

1 bottle (24 fl oz/750 ml) sparkling water, chilled

In a large pitcher, combine the plum and apricot wedges, apricot nectar, orange liqueur, and wine. Stir well, cover, and refrigerate for at least 2 hours or up to 12 hours to blend the flavors.

To serve, fill 4 glasses with ice and add the sangria, dividing it evenly. Top off each glass with sparkling water and serve.

SERVES 4

Kumquat Mojito

3 kumquats, halved

8 fresh mint leaves

Ice

¼ cup (2 fl oz/60 ml) white rum, preferably Myers's

2 Tbsp fresh lime juice

2 Tbsp Simple Syrup (page 250)

Muddle the kumquats and mint leaves in a cocktail shaker. Add ice and the rum, lime juice, and simple syrup, cover, and shake vigorously. Pour the contents, including the fruit and mint, into a Collins glass and serve.

SERVES 1

Cool Drinks for Hot Weather

Nothing beats the heat like an icy-cold beverage—especially when it's mixed with fresh seasonal fruit and herbs. Serve from a pitcher or one at a time.

Mai Tai

¼ cup (2 fl oz/60 ml) Jamaican amber rum

1 Tbsp curaçao

1 Tbsp orgeat syrup

Juice of 1 lime

1 tsp Simple Syrup (page 250)

Ice

Mint sprig

Fill an old-fashioned glass with ice. Fill a cocktail shaker with the rum, curaçao, orgeat syrup, lime juice, and simple syrup. Add ice, cover, shake vigorously, and strain into the ice-filled glass. Garnish with the mint sprig.

SERVES 1

Sparkling Limeade

1 cup (8 fl oz/250 ml) fresh lime juice (from 4 or 5 large limes), plus lime wedges for garnish

6 Tbsp superfine sugar

Ice

1 bottle (24 fl oz/750 ml) sparkling water, chilled

In a large pitcher, combine the lime juice and sugar. Stir until the sugar is dissolved. To serve, fill 4 glasses with ice and add the limeade, dividing it evenly. Top off each glass with sparkling water, garnish with a lime wedge, and serve.

SERVES 4

Grilled Skirt Steak with Chimichurri

Prized for its flavor and ready partnership with the grill, skirt steak is gaining in popularity. It benefits from a long marinade and a quick searing over the fire. Here, it is both marinated and sauced with chimichurri, a classic piquant Argentine condiment. If skirt steak is unavailable, flank steak makes a great substitute.

SERVES 8–10

FOR THE CHIMICHURRI

1 cup (1 oz/30 g) packed fresh flat-leaf parsley leaves and small stems, finely chopped

1 cup (1 oz/30 g) packed fresh cilantro leaves and small stems, finely chopped

¼ small red bell pepper, seeded and finely chopped

3 cloves garlic, minced

2 Tbsp finely chopped yellow onion

½ tsp dried oregano

¼–½ tsp red pepper flakes

1 tsp salt

⅓ cup (3 fl oz/80 ml) extra-virgin olive oil

3 Tbsp sherry vinegar

1 large skirt steak, about 2 lb (1 kg)

2 Tbsp extra-virgin olive oil

To make the chimichurri, in a bowl, combine the parsley, cilantro, bell pepper, garlic, onion, oregano, red pepper flakes, and salt. In a small bowl or cup, whisk together the olive oil and ¼ cup (2 fl oz/60 ml) water; drizzle over the herb mixture and stir well to mix. Let stand at room temperature for about 30 minutes to allow the flavors to blend. (At this point, the sauce can be stored airtight in the refrigerator for up to 2 days. Bring to room temperature before using.)

Pat the steak dry with paper towels. Add the vinegar to the chimichurri and stir to mix well. In a large resealable plastic bag, combine ¼ cup (2 fl oz/60 ml) of the sauce with the oil. Add the steak, seal the bag, and massage to coat the steak with marinade. Let marinate for at least 30 minutes or up to a day.

Prepare a charcoal or gas grill for direct grilling over medium-high heat. Brush and oil the grill grate. Remove the steak from the marinade and place on the grill rack directly over the fire. Grill, turning once, until seared on both sides and medium-rare in the middle, 10–12 minutes total cooking time.

Transfer the steak to a cutting board and let rest for 5 minutes. Cut across the grain into thin slices and arrange on a platter. Just before serving, whisk the chimichurri and spoon over the beef. Serve warm or at room temperature.

final flourish

A grilled cut lemon or lime
makes a nice addition to
the serving platter, and
adds bright flavor to the meat.

Barbecued Baby Back Ribs

Look for meaty ribs with evenly distributed thin streaks of fat for the juiciest, tastiest result. Start the meal with Grilled Shishito Peppers with Sea Salt (page 57) and have plenty of cold beer on hand.

SERVES 4

2 racks baby back pork ribs, about 3 lb (1.5 kg) each

FOR THE CLASSIC RUB

¼ cup (2 oz/60 g) granulated sugar

1 Tbsp firmly packed light brown sugar

¼ cup (1 oz/30 g) paprika

1 Tbsp chili powder

1 tsp cayenne pepper

1 tsp smoked paprika

Salt and freshly ground black pepper

Classic BBQ Sauce (page 249), or 2 cups (16 fl oz/500 ml) BBQ sauce of choice

2 Tbsp honey

Preheat the oven to 300°F (150°C). Remove the membrane from the back of each rack and trim off any excess fat.

To make the rub, in an airtight container, stir together the sugars, paprika, chili powder, cayenne, smoked paprika, 1 teaspoon salt, and several grinds of black pepper. Cover and shake vigorously to mix. Apply the rub to all sides of the racks. Place the ribs side by side on a large piece of aluminum foil and crimp the edges together to seal. Set on a rimmed baking sheet. Bake until the meat is fork tender and just barely starting to shrink away from the bone ends, 2–2½ hours. Remove from the oven and set aside.

Prepare a charcoal or gas grill for direct cooking over medium heat. Brush and oil the grill grate. Grill the ribs, basting with the BBQ sauce and turning frequently, until lacquered, charred in places, and heated through, about 10 minutes. On the last turn, drizzle the honey on the meaty side of the ribs.

Transfer the racks to a cutting board and let rest for about 10 minutes. Cut the racks into individual ribs, pile them on a platter, and serve with the remaining sauce.

Harissa-Rubbed Chicken

Harissa, a spicy red chile condiment from North Africa, gives this chicken both color and flavor. If you are too busy to make your own, purchase the harissa at a North African or well-stocked grocery store.

SERVES 4–6

FOR THE HARISSA

4 dried guajillo chiles

4 dried New Mexican chiles

1½ Tbsp extra-virgin olive oil

1 Tbsp fresh lemon juice

1½ tsp finely chopped garlic

½ tsp ground caraway

½ tsp dried mint

½ tsp salt

¼ tsp ground cumin

¼ tsp freshly ground pepper

1 whole chicken, 3–4 lb (1.5–2 kg), butterflied by your butcher

Put all of the chiles in a large heatproof bowl and add boiling water to cover. Keep the chiles submerged with a small plate and let soak for 1 hour. Protecting your hands with rubber gloves, split the chiles open and swish them in the soaking water to remove most of the seeds. Discard the soaking liquid and seeds.

In a food processor, combine the chiles, oil, lemon juice, garlic, caraway, mint, salt, cumin, and pepper, and process until smooth, stopping to scrape down the sides of the bowl as needed. Transfer the chile mixture to a fine-mesh sieve placed over a bowl and press it through the sieve with a spatula. Discard any solids. Transfer the sauce to an airtight container and set aside.

Place the chicken in a large resealable plastic bag and add 3 tablespoons of the harissa. (Store the remaining harissa for other uses in an airtight container in the refrigerator for up to 1 month.) Seal the bag, massage to coat the chicken, and refrigerate for at least 1 hour or up to 48 hours. Remove the chicken from the refrigerator 30 minutes before grilling.

Prepare a charcoal or gas grill for indirect grilling over medium heat; the temperature inside the grill should be 350°–375°F (180°–190°C). If using charcoal, bank the lit coals on one side of the grill bed, and place a drip pan in the area without coals. If using gas, preheat the burners, then turn off one or more of the burners to create a cooler zone. Brush and oil the grill grate.

Place the chicken, skin side up, on the cooler part of the grill and cook for 15 minutes. Turn and continue cooking until an instant-read thermometer inserted into the thickest part of a thigh away from the bone registers 170°F (77°C), or the juices run clear when a thigh joint is pierced with a knife tip, about 15 minutes longer. Transfer the chicken to a cutting board, tent with aluminum foil, and let rest for 10 minutes. Cut into serving pieces and serve.

handy eats

Skewers are terrific tools for hosts, essential for preparing main dishes like this spicy chicken, but also useful for grilling bite-size vegetable chunks or creating stacked tropical fruit sticks for dessert.

Tandoori-Style Chicken Kebabs

For this stress-free recipe, the chicken is marinated overnight, leaving only firing up the grill, loading the skewers, and grilling them for serving day. Pair them with plain or coconut rice (page 84), a simple salad, and mango ice pops (page 100) for dessert.

SERVES 6

FOR THE TANDOORI MARINADE

2 cups (1 lb/500 g) plain whole-milk yogurt

2 Tbsp fresh lemon juice

2 Tbsp peeled and minced fresh ginger

4 cloves garlic, minced

1 tsp ground coriander

1 tsp ground turmeric

½ tsp saffron threads

½ tsp ground cumin

½ tsp cayenne pepper

Salt and freshly ground black pepper

6–12 metal or wood skewers

8 boneless, skinless chicken thighs

2–3 lemons, sliced (optional)

1 small red onion, thinly sliced and separated into rings (optional)

¼ cup (⅓ oz/10 g) chopped fresh cilantro

To make the tandoori marinade, in a bowl, whisk together the yogurt, lemon juice, ginger, garlic, coriander, turmeric, saffron, cumin, cayenne, 1 teaspoon salt, and ½ teaspoon black pepper.

Cut the chicken thighs into 1-inch (2.5-cm) cubes. Place the chicken cubes in a large resealable plastic bag and pour in the marinade. Seal the bag, massage to coat the chicken, and refrigerate overnight.

At least 30 minutes before grilling, remove the chicken from the refrigerator. Discard the marinade. If using wood skewers, soak in water for 30 minutes. Prepare a charcoal or gas grill for direct grilling over high heat. Brush and oil the grill grate.

Thread the chicken cubes onto the skewers without crowding them, alternating the chicken with the lemon slices, if using. Place the skewers on the grill directly over the fire and cook, turning once, until the chicken is lightly grill-marked on both sides and opaque throughout but still moist, about 5 minutes per side. If the chicken begins to burn, move the skewers to the edge of a charcoal grill or lower the heat of a gas grill.

Slide the chicken off the skewers onto a platter. Top with the onion (if using) and the cilantro and serve.

THE ALFRESCO TABLE

FIND INSPIRATION *in what's seasonal and fresh to set*

a memorable scene for your outdoor get-together.

Source fragrant herbs and flowers **FROM YOUR GARDEN**

or a local supplier, and seek out unique containers like

galvanized tin buckets, mason jars in a mix of sizes,

or colorful ceramic pitchers. Mix high- and low-light candles

and play with an **ECLECTIC MIX** *of dishes and glassware*

until you find a look that expresses **YOUR PERSONAL STYLE.**

ice cream sandwiches

Place a scoop of ice cream between two homemade or store-bought chocolate wafers and press down gently to form a sandwich. For a special treat, roll the edges of the sandwich in miniature chocolate chips.

Chocolate-Flecked Mint Ice Cream

Using fresh mint as opposed to mint extract adds bright flavor to this ice cream. Instead of large chocolate chunks, which can be both hard to bite into and difficult to scoop, the chocolate is finely grated, creating thin shards that melt easily in your mouth.

MAKES ABOUT 1 QUART (1 L)

1¾ cups (14 fl oz/430 ml) heavy cream

1½ cups (12 fl oz/375 ml) whole milk

¾ cup (¾ oz/20 g) fresh mint leaves

4 large egg yolks

¾ cup (6 oz/185 g) sugar

⅛ tsp salt

2 drops green food coloring (optional)

5 oz (155 g) bittersweet chocolate, finely grated

In a heavy saucepan, combine the cream, milk, and mint leaves. Warm over medium-high heat, stirring occasionally, until the mixture barely simmers, about 5 minutes.

Meanwhile, in a heatproof bowl, combine the egg yolks, sugar, and salt. Whisk vigorously until the mixture lightens in color and doubles in volume, about 2 minutes.

Remove the cream mixture from the heat. Whisking constantly, slowly pour about 1 cup (8 fl oz/250 ml) of the warm cream mixture into the egg mixture and whisk until smooth. Pour the resulting egg-cream mixture back into the saucepan over medium heat, whisking constantly. Using a wooden spoon, stir until the mixture forms a custard thick enough to coat the back of the spoon, 1–2 minutes. Do not let the mixture boil.

Meanwhile, have ready an ice bath in a large bowl, and nest a smaller heatproof bowl inside. Pour the custard through a fine-mesh sieve into the smaller bowl, stirring occasionally until cool. Remove the bowl from the ice bath, stir in the food coloring, if using, and cover with plastic wrap. Refrigerate until very cold, at least 4 hours or up to 3 days.

Pour the cold custard into an ice cream maker and churn according to the manufacturer's instructions. Add the grated chocolate during the last minute of churning. Spoon the ice cream into an airtight freezer-safe container and place parchment or waxed paper directly on the surface. Cover tightly and freeze until firm, at least 2 hours or up to 3 days.

Ice Pops Six Ways

watermelon + mint

2 cups (10 oz/315 g) watermelon chunks
or fresh strawberries

1 Tbsp sugar

1 Tbsp fresh lime juice

2–3 sprigs fresh mint

In a blender, combine the watermelon, sugar, and lime juice. Process until smooth, adding enough water to make the mixture pourable. Remove the leaves from the mint springs, add them to the watermelon mixture, and stir gently. Divide the mixture among 5–6 ice pop molds. Freeze until solid.

lemon verbena + blueberry

⅔ cup (5 oz/155 g) sugar

4 small sprigs lemon verbena

1 Tbsp fresh lemon juice

1¼ cups (5 oz/165 g) blueberries

In a small saucepan, combine the sugar and 1 cup (8 fl oz/250 ml) water. Add the lemon verbena leaves. Bring to a boil over medium-high heat, stirring often, until the sugar has dissolved, 3–4 minutes. Let cool. Stir in the lemon juice. In a blender, combine ⅓ cup (3 fl oz/80 ml) of the lemon syrup (no leaves) with the blueberries. Process until smooth. Divide the remaining lemon syrup among 6 ice pop molds. Freeze until semi-hard, add the blueberry mixture, and freeze until solid.

mango + pistachio

⅓ cup (3 oz/90 g) sugar

2 cups (12 oz/375 g) diced mango

2 Tbsp fresh lime juice

½ cup (2½ oz/75 g) finely chopped
toasted and salted pistachios

In a small saucepan, combine the sugar, and ½ cup (4 fl oz/125 ml) water. Bring to a boil over medium-high heat, stirring often, until the sugar has dissolved, 3–4 minutes. Let cool. In a blender, combine the mango, lime juice, and cooled syrup. Process until smooth. Divide the mango mixture equally among 8 ice pop molds. Freeze until solid. Dip unmolded pops into the pistachios.

Nothing cools down a hot day like homemade ice pops. Use purchased ice pop molds or sturdy paper cups for freezing the pops. To keep sticks upright in the liquid, cover the cups with aluminum foil and poke the sticks through the top. To release the popsicles, run the molds under warm water for 30 seconds.

plum
+
orange

1 cup (8 fl oz/250 ml) fresh orange juice
5 Tbsp honey
Pinch of salt
3 black plums, cut into wedges

In a bowl, stir together the orange juice, honey, and salt. Add ¼ cup (2 fl oz/60 ml) plus 2 tablespoons water and stir to combine. Fill 6 ice pop molds about halfway with the orange juice mixture, add a few wedges of plum to each mold, and freeze until semi-hard. Add the remaining plums and juice mixture to each mold and freeze until solid.

chai
+
cacao nibs

¾ cup (6 oz/185 g) sugar
2 chai tea bags
¾ cup (6 fl oz/180 ml) whole milk
⅓ cup (3 oz/90 g) cacao nibs

In a saucepan, combine the sugar and 2 cups (16 fl oz/500 ml) water. Add the tea bags and bring to a simmer over medium-high heat, stirring often, until the sugar has dissolved, 3–4 minutes. Add the milk. Let steep for 10 minutes. Divide the mixture among 8–10 ice pop molds. Freeze until solid. Dip unmolded pops into cacoa nibs.

lime
+
honeydew melon

½ cup (4 oz/125g) sugar
2 strips lime zest and lime juice to taste
1 honeydew melon, seeded, peeled, and diced (about 4 cups/1½ lb/750 g)

In a small saucepan, combine the sugar, lime zest, and ½ cup (4 fl oz/125 ml) water. Bring to a boil over medium-high heat, stirring often, until the sugar dissolves, 3–4 minutes. Let cool. Remove the zest and pour into a blender. Add the melon and process until smooth. Add lime juice to taste. Divide among 8–10 ice pop molds. Freeze until solid.

Grilled Peaches with Cardamom Cream

Stone fruit seared on a hot grill and topped with whipped cream is one of the best ways to end a summer meal—and also one of the easiest. You can trade out the cardamom for cinnamon or ginger or for a splash of vanilla extract.

SERVES 4–8

3 Tbsp honey

1 Tbsp brandy or fruit-based liqueur

½ tsp ground cardamom

4 firm-ripe peaches, halved and pitted

Olive oil for brushing

½ cup (4 fl oz/125 ml) cold heavy cream

In a bowl, combine the honey, brandy, and ¼ teaspoon of the cardamom. Whisk briskly to loosen the honey and mix well. Add the peach halves and toss gently to coat. Cover and set aside.

Prepare a charcoal or gas grill for direct grilling over high heat. Brush and oil the grill grate.

Meanwhile, in a chilled metal or glass bowl, using an electric mixer set on medium speed, beat the cream until soft peaks form, about 4 minutes. Add the remaining ¼ teaspoon cardamom and beat until fluffy, stiff peaks form, 1–2 minutes longer. Cover and refrigerate until ready to serve.

Using tongs, remove the peach halves from the honey mixture and arrange, cut sides down, on the grill rack directly over the fire, reserving the remaining honey mixture. Cook the peach halves until tender and grill-marked, 3–4 minutes.

Transfer the peaches to a platter or individual plates and let cool slightly. Serve warm, topped with the whipped cream and drizzled with the reserved honey mixture.

Strawberry-Hazelnut Shortcakes

You can bake the biscuits early in the day and leave them, covered, on the countertop until dinnertime. They are delicate, so use a serrated knife and a gentle sawing motion to split them—or serve them whole with a big scoop of the berries topped with whipped cream alongside.

SERVES 6

1½ cups (7½ oz/235 g) all-purpose flour

⅓ cup (2½ oz/75 g) firmly packed light brown sugar

2 tsp baking powder

½ tsp salt

6 Tbsp (3 oz/90 g) cold unsalted butter, cut into 6 pieces

⅔ cup (3 oz/90 g) toasted hazelnuts

½ cup (4 fl oz/125 ml) cold heavy cream, plus more for brushing

Turbinado sugar for sprinkling

2 lb (1 kg) strawberries

1 rounded Tbsp granulated sugar

¼ tsp dried lavender flowers

2 Tbsp honey

Vanilla Whipped Cream (page 250)

Preheat the oven to 400°F (200°C). Line a large, heavy baking sheet with parchment paper.

In a food processor, combine the flour, brown sugar, baking powder, and salt and pulse a few times to mix. Scatter the butter over the flour mixture and pulse until the mixture resembles coarse cornmeal. Add the hazelnuts and pulse until the hazelnuts are finely chopped. Pour the cream evenly over the mixture and pulse until moist clumps form.

Remove the dough from the processor, gather into a ball, and transfer to a lightly floured work surface. Pat the dough into a 4-by-6-inch (10-by-15-cm) rectangle. Using a sharp knife, cut the rectangle into 2-inch (5-cm) squares, making 6 biscuits total without scraps.

Transfer the biscuits to the prepared baking sheet. Brush the tops with cream and sprinkle with turbinado sugar. Bake the biscuits until golden brown and cooked through, about 14 minutes. Let cool on the baking sheet on a wire rack.

Meanwhile, prepare the strawberries: Core the strawberries, then halve the small ones or quarter the large ones lengthwise. Place in a large bowl. In a mortar, using a pestle, grind together the granulated sugar and lavender until the lavender is finely ground. Sprinkle the lavender sugar over the strawberries, then drizzle with the honey, stirring to coat the berries evenly.

Split each biscuit and place on individual plates. Spoon the berries and whipped cream onto the bottom halves, cap with the tops, and serve.

Fruity Hand Pies

Have plenty of napkins ready for these handheld pies, as part of their appeal is the delicious fruit juice that escapes with every bite. They are easily portable, so pack them for a picnic, or arrange them in a basket for a grab-and-go dessert at a casual barbecue.

SERVES 6

Double-Crust Flaky Pie Dough
(page 248)

FOR THE BLUEBERRY FILLING

2 cups (8 oz/250 g) blueberries

¼ cup (2 oz/60 g) granulated sugar

1 Tbsp fresh lemon juice

2 tsp cornstarch

FOR THE APPLE-CINNAMON FILLING

4 baking apples, peeled, cored,
and cut into small chunks
(scant 3 cups/12 oz/375 g)

Juice of ¼ lemon

⅓ cup (2½ oz/75 g) firmly packed
light brown sugar

¼ tsp ground cinnamon

1 Tbsp all-purpose flour

1 large egg, beaten with 1 tsp water

1 Tbsp granulated sugar

Prepare the dough and chill as directed. Make the filling of choice:

To make the blueberry filling, combine 1½ cups (6 oz/185 g) of the blueberries, the sugar, and the lemon juice in a saucepan over medium heat. Cook, stirring frequently, until the berries begin to give off their juices. Reduce the heat to medium-low and simmer, stirring occasionally, until all of the berries have burst, about 5 minutes. In a small bowl, stir together the cornstarch and 2 tablespoons water. Add the cornstarch mixture to the blueberry mixture and cook until the juices come to a boil and thicken. Remove from the heat and stir in the remaining ½ cup berries. Place the saucepan in a bowl of ice water to cool quickly, stirring frequently. Set aside.

To make the apple-cinnamon filling, in a medium bowl, combine the apple chunks, lemon juice, brown sugar, cinnamon, and flour.

Preheat the oven to 375°F (190°C). Place one of the dough disks on a lightly floured work surface. Cut the disk into 3 equal pieces. Dust the top of each piece with flour and roll each piece into a round about 5 inches (13 cm) in diameter and ⅛ inch (3 mm) thick. Trim the edges to make a perfect circle. Repeat with the remaining dough disk.

Place 3 rounds on an ungreased rimmed baking sheet. Divide half the filling among them, spooning it in the center of each and leaving ½ inch (12 mm) uncovered around the edge. Brush the dough edge with egg wash and fold the round over to create a half moon, pressing the edges together. Using a fork, crimp the edge to seal completely. Refrigerate the pies while you repeat the process with the remaining dough and filling, and place the remaining pies on the same baking sheet. Refrigerate for 15 minutes.

Lightly brush the pies with egg wash, and sprinkle with the 1 tablespoon sugar. Bake until golden brown at the edges, about 20 minutes. Let cool on a rack, then serve.

versatile pies

Stone fruits, when in season, also make a nice filling for these pies. Swap in 1½ cups (6 oz/185 g) finely chopped plums, peaches, or apricots for the blueberries.

CHAPTER THREE

DINNER PARTIES

Food tastes better with friends

Fresh Fig, Goat Cheese & Mint Flatbread

Peak season for figs generally stretches from midsummer to early fall. Black Mission is the most common variety, but other types, such as Brown Turkey or the yellowish-green Kadota, will also work in this enticing recipe. Pomegranate seeds add extra color, flavor, and crunch.

SERVES 8–10

Flatbread Dough (page 248)
or 1 lb (500 g) purchased
pizza dough

Olive oil for brushing

FOR THE HONEY-BALSAMIC VINAIGRETTE

1 Tbsp balsamic vinegar

½ tsp honey

Salt and freshly ground pepper

1½–2 Tbsp olive oil

6 oz (180 g) goat cheese

1 pint (10 oz/315 g) fresh figs, halved

¼ cup (1¼ oz/35 g) pomegranate seeds

Fresh mint leaves and oregano leaves for garnish

Salt and freshly ground pepper

Honey for drizzling

Place the homemade or purchased dough on a lightly floured work surface and press flat to release excess air. (If the dough has risen in the refrigerator, cover with a kitchen towel and bring to room temperature before continuing.)

Preheat the oven to 425°F (220°C). Grease a baking sheet with olive oil. Press and stretch the dough into a rough oval about 10 by 20 inches (25 by 50 cm). Transfer to the prepared baking sheet and brush liberally with olive oil. Bake for 8 minutes.

Meanwhile, make the honey-balsamic vinaigrette: In a bowl, whisk together the vinegar, honey, and a pinch each of salt and pepper. Whisking constantly, slowly add the oil until emulsified. Set aside.

Crumble the goat cheese over the flatbread, then arrange the figs evenly over the top. Continue to bake until the flatbread is golden, 6–8 minutes longer.

Sprinkle the pomegranate seeds over the flatbread, then garnish with mint and oregano leaves. Drizzle the vinaigrette over the top, season to taste with salt and pepper, then finish with a drizzle of honey. Cut into pieces and serve.

variation

MEDITERRANEAN FLATBREAD
Brush the flatbread dough lightly with olive oil, then layer with a mix of sliced and whole tomatoes, thin slabs of feta cheese, and pitted Kalamata olives. Bake until the crust is golden, about 15 minutes. Sprinkle with fresh thyme and oregano just before serving.

tailor-made

Flatbread is a versatile appetizer
for entertaining and allows for
mix-and-match toppings, depending
on the season. Consider fresh
fruit in summer or prosciutto and
caramelized onions in winter.

A GRACIOUS WELCOME *Be ready to offer cold drinks and simple hors d'oeuvres when guests arrive. With soft music playing, candles already lit, and ice and cocktail napkins at the ready, the stage will be set for a festive evening.*

Serving Cheese Four Ways

goat cheese + chutney

½ cup (4 oz/125 g) spiced stone fruit chutney (page 249)
1 wedge (6 oz/180 g) St. André or goat cheese
¼ cup (1 oz/30 g) toasted, salted pistachios, chopped
Table water or thyme-flecked crackers for serving

Spoon chutney into a small bowl. Place the bowl on a platter with the goat cheese. Sprinkle pistachios over the cheese. Serve with crackers.

parmesan + radish + apple

1 wedge (6 oz/180 g) good-quality Parmesan or dry Jack cheese
2 watermelon radishes • 1 apple, cored and cut into thin wedges
½ cup (2½ oz/75 g) marcona almonds • Salted crackers for serving

Using a cheese plane, shave the cheese into thin slices and arrange on a serving plate. Using a mandoline or serrated vegetable peeler, shave the radishes into thin slices. Mound the radishes on the plate with the cheese and add the apple wedges. Place the almonds in a small bowl and serve alongside. Serve with crackers.

A well-curated cheese platter is a thing of beauty, and a big draw at a party. Set out a short, pointed blade for hard cheese, a curved spreader for soft cheese, and a wide blade for semihard cheese, and count on 1 to 1½ oz (30 to 45 g) of cheese per person.

burrata + figs

½ lb (250 g) burrata cheese • Extra-virgin olive oil for drizzling • Coarse salt and freshly ground pepper 1 pint (10 oz/315 g) fresh Mission or Kadota figs, halved Fresh basil leaves for garnish • Crostini for serving

Place the burrata in a bowl. Drizzle with olive oil and sprinkle with salt and pepper. Place the bowl on a serving plate alongside the figs. Sprinkle the plate with basil leaves. Serve with crostini.

gorgonzola + honeycomb

1 wedge (6 oz/180 g) gorgonzola or Stilton cheese 4 oz (125 g) honeycomb • ½ cup (2 oz/60 g) pomegranate seeds 1 baguette, sliced, or whole-wheat crackers for serving

Place the gorgonzola on a serving plate alongside the honeycomb. Sprinkle pomegranate seeds over the plate. Serve with sliced baguette or crackers.

Orange-Glazed Roasted Beets

Earthy beets, tangy goat cheese, fresh herbs, and tart orange team up in this colorful dish for fall and winter menus. All of the components— the roasted beets, the seasoned yogurt, the dressing—can be prepared in advance and then combined just before serving.

SERVES 4–6

1 orange

6 beets, about 1½ lb (750 g) total weight, greens removed

3 Tbsp extra-virgin olive oil, plus more for drizzling

2 cloves garlic

Salt and freshly ground pepper

½ cup (4 oz/125 g) plain whole-milk Greek yogurt

1½ tsp minced fresh chives

1 Tbsp shelled roasted pistachios

Preheat the oven to 400°F (200°C).

Finely shred 1 teaspoon of zest from the orange and set aside. Halve the orange, place half in a baking dish just large enough to hold it and the beets in a single layer, and set the other half aside. Add the beets to the baking dish and drizzle with 2 tablespoons of the olive oil. Add the garlic, sprinkle lightly with salt and pepper, and toss well to coat. Cover the dish with foil and roast until the beets are tender when pierced with a paring knife, about 45 minutes. Remove the beets from the oven and let cool.

Spoon the yogurt into a small bowl. Stir in the zest and 1 tablespoon of juice from the reserved fresh orange half; set the orange aside. Season to taste with salt. Cover and refrigerate until ready to serve.

Using the dull side of the paring knife, gently scrape the skins off the beets, then cut into a mix of wedges, halves, and slices. Arrange the beets in a bowl or on a platter.

Squeeze the juice from the roasted orange half into a small bowl and whisk in the remaining 1 tablespoon oil to make a dressing. Squeeze in more juice from the reserved fresh orange half, if desired, and let the dressing cool to room temperature.

Drizzle the beets lightly with the dressing, then sprinkle lightly with salt and pepper. Sprinkle the chives and pistachios over the yogurt mixture, then drizzle lightly with olive oil. Serve the beets alongside the yogurt mixture for spooning on top.

A traditional cooking method that is easy to master, roasting is a great choice for entertaining. For everything from leg of lamb to root vegetables, the time in the oven yields tender interiors and rich caramelized exteriors and frees you up for other hosting duties.

Grilled Salt & Pepper Shrimp

Pair the spiced shrimp with a sweet and fruity Grilled Pineapple Salsa (page 72)—the marriage of salty and sweet is sublime. For a more classic partnership, serve it with Garlic-Lemon Butter (page 194), Romesco (page 69), or Saffron Aioli (page 249).

SERVES 6–8

4 lb (2 kg) large shrimp, peeled and thawed if frozen

2 Tbsp fresh lime juice

1 Tbsp coarse salt

1 Tbsp cracked black pepper from whole peppercorns (see note)

1 Tbsp cracked white pepper from whole peppercorns (see note)

1 tsp cayenne pepper

½ tsp chili powder

1 splash dry vermouth

¼ cup (2 fl oz/60 ml) olive oil

Salsa of choice (page 72)

Place the shrimp in a colander, rinse under cold running water, and pat dry with paper towels. In a large bowl, combine the shrimp, lime juice, salt, black pepper, white pepper, cayenne, and chile powder and toss to coat. Add the splash of vermouth and the olive oil and toss to coat. Cover and refrigerate until ready to use.

Prepare a charcoal or gas grill for direct grilling over medium-high heat. Brush and oil the grill grate. (Alternatively, preheat a stove-top grill pan over medium-high heat.)

Working in batches, grill the shrimp directly over the fire, turning once, until bright red and grill-marked, 2–3 minutes per side. Place the cooked shrimp on a platter and tent with foil to keep warm. When all the shrimp are grilled, serve with salsa for dipping.

cracking peppercorns

To crack whole peppercorns, lay a large sheet of parchment paper or waxed paper on a cutting board that sits firmly on a work surface. Place 2–3 tablespoons peppercorns in the center and fold the edges over to make a small pouch. Using a heavy sauté pan or Dutch oven, apply pressure and rock back and forth to crack the peppercorns. Strain through a coarse-mesh sieve into a bowl and repeat the process until most of the peppercorns are cracked.

Roasted Baby Artichokes with Aioli

Roasting artichokes brings out their natural nuttiness and sweetness. Here, they are paired with aioli, a mayonnaise-based dipping sauce flavored with aromatic saffron and sweet-tart Meyer lemon juice. If you cannot find a Meyer lemon, use a regular one instead.

SERVES 6–8

1 large Meyer lemon

2 lb (1 kg) baby artichokes

¼ cup (2 fl oz/60 ml) extra-virgin olive oil

Salt and freshly ground pepper

Pinch of saffron threads

¼ cup (2 fl oz/60 ml) mayonnaise

1 clove garlic, minced

Preheat the oven to 425°F (220°C). Line a rimmed baking sheet with foil. Bring a large pot three-fourths full of water to a boil over high heat.

Halve the lemon, squeeze 1 tablespoon juice, and set the juice aside. Fill a large bowl three-fourths full with water and squeeze the juice from the remaining lemon half into the water. Working with 1 artichoke at a time, snap off the dark green outer leaves until you reach the tender, pale-green inner leaves. Cut off the stem flush with the bottom and discard, and cut off about ½ inch (12 mm) from the top of the artichoke to remove the spiny tips. Cut the artichoke in half lengthwise and drop the halves into the lemon water to prevent discoloration. Repeat with the remaining artichokes.

Drain the artichokes, add them to the boiling water, and cook until just tender when pierced with a knife, about 5 minutes. Drain well in a colander and let cool slightly.

In a bowl, combine the warm artichokes, olive oil, and a light sprinkle of salt and pepper and toss to coat evenly. Pour in a single layer onto the prepared baking sheet. Roast until the artichokes turn brown on the bottom and edges, 10–15 minutes.

Meanwhile, to make the aioli, in a small bowl, soak the saffron in 1 tablespoon hot water for about 5 minutes. In another bowl, combine the mayonnaise, garlic, and reserved lemon juice and mix well. Stir in the saffron with its soaking water, mixing well. Season to taste with salt.

Remove the artichokes from the oven and let cool slightly. Arrange on a serving platter with the aioli and serve.

spanish specialty

Marcona almonds, imported from Spain, are an excellent pantry item because they are both a great addition to recipes and an elegant nibble for cocktail hour.

Citrus Salad with Mint & Marcona Almonds

Put this salad on a dinner menu in winter, when citrus fruits are at their best. You can use white or pink grapefruits, navel or blood oranges, or a mixture. The fruits can be combined with the dressing up to two hours in advance and left at cool room temperature.

SERVES 8

1 Tbsp honey

1 Tbsp fresh orange juice

½ tsp fresh lemon juice

2 Tbsp minced fresh mint, plus leaves for garnish

3 grapefruits

3 oranges

12 kumquats

8 butter lettuce leaves

¼ cup (1½ oz/45 g) Marcona almonds, chopped

Pomegranate seeds for garnish (optional)

Edible flowers for garnish (optional)

In a large bowl, combine the honey, orange juice, lemon juice, and minced mint and mix well with a fork or whisk.

Working with 1 grapefruit at a time, using a sharp knife, cut a slice off both ends of the grapefruit to reveal the flesh. Stand the grapefruit upright on a cutting board and cut downward to remove the peel and white pith. Holding the grapefruit in one hand over a bowl, cut along both sides of each segment to release it from the membrane, letting the segments and juice drop into the bowl. Remove any seeds, and add to the honey mixture along with the juice. Repeat with the oranges. Thinly slice the kumquats, remove the seeds, and add to the bowl with the citrus. Gently turn the fruit to coat with the dressing.

Place a lettuce leaf on each salad plate and divide the fruit among them, or arrange the leaves on a serving plate and spoon the citrus over the top. Sprinkle with the almonds, garnish with the pomegranate seeds and edible flowers (if using), and serve.

Shaken Cocktails

When you're having a party, the chattering of a cocktail shaker signals celebration and conviviality like little else. Each one of these recipes makes enough to serve two, so keep mixing and shaking if you're tending a crowd.

Jack Rose

Ice • 4 fl oz (125 ml) applejack or other apple brandy
1½ fl oz (45 ml) grenadine • 2 fl oz (60 ml) fresh lime juice
2 edible blossoms

Fill a cocktail shaker a third full with ice. Add the applejack, grenadine, and the lime juice. Cover, shake vigorously, and strain into 2 chilled martini glasses. Garnish with the blossoms and serve.

Dirty Martini

Ice • 5 fl oz (125 ml) vodka or gin • 1 fl oz (30 ml) brine
from a jar of olives • 2 dashes dry vermouth • 4 martini olives

Fill a cocktail shaker a third full with ice. Add the vodka, brine, and vermouth. Cover, shake vigorously, and strain into 2 chilled martini glasses. Garnish with the olives and serve.

Elderflower Gin Fizz

Ice • 4 fl oz (125 ml) gin • 2 fl oz (60 ml) St. Germain
elderflower liqueur • 1½ fl oz (45 ml) pink grapefruit juice
2 egg whites • Sparkling water • Fresh currant sprigs

Fill a cocktail shaker a third full with ice. Add the gin,
elderflower liqueur, grapefruit juice, and the egg whites.
Cover and shake vigorously. Strain into 2 stemmed
glasses and top with sparkling water. Garnish with
fresh currant sprigs and serve.

Blueberry-Verbena Collins

½ cup (2 oz/60 g) fresh blueberries • 2 fresh lemon verbena
leaves, plus leaves for garnish • ⅓ cup (3 oz/90 g) sugar
2 tablespoons water • Ice • 4 fl oz (125 ml) vodka • Sparkling water

Combine the berries, 2 verbena leaves, sugar, and water
in a saucepan. Bring to a boil, then reduce heat and simmer
for 2 minutes. Let cool. Fill a cocktail shaker a third full with
ice. Add 2 fl oz (60 ml) of the syrup and the vodka. Cover
and shake vigorously. Pour into 2 glasses and top with
sparkling water. Garnish with verbena leaves and serve.

EASY ENTERTAINING

If you like **CASUAL GATHERINGS**, *keep things*

simple by inviting guests to help themselves.

Serve flatbread topped with **SEASONAL PRODUCE**

picked out that morning at your local farmers' market.

Offer several **DIFFERENT WINES** *that complement*

the food and encourage sampling, always progressing

from lighter whites to heavier reds over the course

of the evening. Skipping the formalities means

more time to **RELAX AND ENJOY THE PARTY**.

Warm Kale Salad with Crispy Bacon & Egg

Shredding and briefly blanching kale for a salad softens its sturdy texture, but keeps it crunchy enough to support hearty, heavier ingredients like hard-boiled eggs and pancetta. The kale can be left raw, too, for a crunchier effect.

SERVES 4–5

5 large eggs

2 bunches kale

Salt and freshly ground black pepper

¼ lb (125 g) thick-cut bacon or pancetta, coarsely chopped

3 Tbsp extra-virgin olive oil

1 clove garlic, minced

¼ cup (2 fl oz/60 ml) balsamic vinegar

2 Tbsp red wine vinegar

¼ cup (⅓ oz/10 g) chopped fresh flat-leaf parsley leaves

½ tsp cayenne pepper

Place the eggs in a saucepan just large enough to hold them. Add cold water to cover by 1 inch (2.5 cm) and bring just to a boil over high heat. Remove the pan from the heat and cover. Let stand for 15 minutes. Have ready a bowl of ice water. Drain the eggs, then place in the ice water and let cool before peeling. Chop the eggs and set aside.

Using a knife, cut the ribs from the kale and discard, then roll up the leaves and slice them thinly crosswise. Fill a large saucepan three-fourths full of water and bring to a boil over medium-high heat. Add 1 teaspoon salt and the kale and cook until the greens are just tender, about 5 minutes. Drain the kale in a colander in the sink, then rinse under cold running water until cool. Drain again, gently squeeze out the excess liquid from the kale, then coarsely chop it. Gently squeeze out the liquid again. Set aside.

In a frying pan over medium heat, cook the pancetta, turning occasionally, until nearly golden, about 5 minutes. (If using bacon, pour off the rendered fat.) Add 1 tablespoon of the olive oil and the garlic and cook just until the garlic is golden, about 1 minute. Using a slotted spoon, place the pancetta and garlic on paper towels to drain.

Add 2 tablespoons of the balsamic vinegar to the same frying pan and cook over medium heat, stirring to scrape up any browned bits on the pan bottom. Pour into a bowl and whisk in the remaining 2 tablespoons balsamic vinegar, the red wine vinegar, and the remaining 2 tablespoons olive oil. Add the kale, the pancetta and garlic, 3 tablespoons of the parsley, and ½ teaspoon black pepper. Mix well. Gently fold in the chopped eggs. Garnish with the remaining 1 tablespoon parsley and the cayenne and serve.

Balsamic-Braised Beef Short Ribs

Since short ribs are best when simmered long and slow, make this dish when you're feeling like a homebody. Serve the tender meat over creamy polenta or steamed rice in shallow bowls. Leftovers keep in the refrigerator for up to 3 days or in the freezer for up to 1 month.

SERVES 6–8

4–5 lb (2–2.5 kg) bone-in beef short ribs, each about 3 inches (7.5 cm) long

Salt and freshly ground pepper

1 Tbsp olive oil

⅔ cup (5 fl oz/160 ml) balsamic vinegar

½ cup (4 fl oz/125 ml) dry red wine

2 Tbsp tomato paste

1 yellow onion, thinly sliced

6 cloves garlic, crushed

10 sprigs fresh flat-leaf parsley plus ¼ cup (¼ oz/7 g) lightly packed fresh parsley leaves, chopped, for garnish

2 bay leaves

Trim any excess fat from the short ribs, but leave the silver skin and connective tissue intact. Arrange the ribs in a single layer in a baking dish. Sprinkle with 1–2 tablespoons salt and cover loosely with plastic wrap. Refrigerate for at least 3 hours or up to overnight.

Remove the ribs from the refrigerator and pat dry with paper towels. In a large, heavy frying pan over medium heat, warm the olive oil. Working in batches to avoid crowding, place the ribs in the pan and sear, turning once, until they develop a golden crust on both sides, about 4 minutes per side. As each batch is done, place in a Dutch oven or a slow cooker.

Add the vinegar, wine, tomato paste, onion, garlic, parsley sprigs, and bay leaves to the meat and stir to combine. Cover and cook over low heat for 4–6 hours. Uncover after 4 hours and check one of the thickest ribs to see if the meat is very tender and falling off the bone. If not, cover and continue cooking, checking again about every 30 minutes.

Using a slotted spoon, transfer the ribs to a platter or large, shallow serving bowl. Discard the parsley sprigs and bay leaves.

Using a large spoon, skim off any fat from the surface of the cooking liquid and discard. Pour the cooking liquid into a saucepan and place over medium heat, reserving the onion in the cooker. Simmer the cooking liquid until reduced to about ¾ cup (6 fl oz/180 ml), about 10 minutes. Taste and adjust the seasoning.

Spoon the sauce around the ribs. Top with a few spoonfuls of the onion from the pot, garnish with the chopped parsley, and serve.

Roast Chicken with Potatoes & Carrots

A whole chicken roasted with vegetables makes a comforting dinner.
In this version, the bird is flavored with tarragon and thyme,
with tender spring potatoes and carrots tucked alongside.

SERVES 4

2 Tbsp olive oil, plus more for greasing

1 chicken, about 4 lb (2 kg), giblets removed

4 sprigs *each* fresh tarragon and fresh thyme

4 tsp *each* minced fresh tarragon and fresh thyme, plus more for garnish

Coarse kosher salt and freshly ground pepper

2 lb (1 kg) small potatoes, each about 2 inches (5 cm) in diameter, halved

2 lb (1 kg) baby carrots, trimmed

2–3 heads garlic, unpeeled, sliced or left whole

½ cup (4 fl oz/125 ml) dry white wine

Preheat the oven to 450°F (230°C). Grease a large, heavy rimmed baking sheet (not a roasting pan). Pat the chicken dry with paper towels. Starting at the edge of the main cavity, slide a finger under the skin over each breast half, making 2 pockets. Place 1 sprig tarragon and 1 sprig thyme in each pocket. Sprinkle the chicken with 1½ teaspoons each of the minced tarragon and minced thyme and season with salt and pepper. Place the remaining 2 sprigs tarragon and 2 sprigs thyme into the main cavity. Place the chicken on the prepared baking sheet and roast for 30 minutes.

Meanwhile, in a large bowl, toss the potatoes, carrots, and garlic with the olive oil to coat. Add 2 teaspoons each of the minced tarragon and minced thyme. Sprinkle lightly with salt and pepper and toss to coat.

Remove the chicken from the oven. Tilt the sheet and spoon off most of the fat. Place the chicken in the center of the baking sheet and spoon the vegetables around it, turning the potatoes cut side down. Continue roasting until an instant-read thermometer inserted into the thickest part of a thigh registers 165°F (74°C), about 40 minutes longer. Transfer the potatoes, carrots, and garlic to a warmed platter. Using a kitchen towel, lift the bird and tip it, letting the juices run into a small, heavy saucepan. Place the chicken on the platter alongside the vegetables.

Pour the juices from the baking sheet into the saucepan. Using a spoon, skim off any fat from the top and discard. Place the baking sheet over medium heat, add the wine, and deglaze the pan, stirring to remove any browned bits from the pan bottom. Pour the pan juices into the saucepan. Boil until reduced slightly, about 5 minutes. Add any accumulated juices from the chicken platter. Mix the remaining ½ teaspoon each minced tarragon and minced thyme into the sauce. Taste and adjust the seasoning. Garnish with minced tarragon and thyme. Carve the chicken and serve with the vegetables and sauce.

Filets Mignons with Watercress & Parmesan Butter

Here, filet mignon, one of the most lauded cuts of beef, is cooked first on the stove top, then finished in the oven. The Parmesan butter melts over the warm meat, complementing its richness and adding an appealing nuttiness. Don't be tempted to use a nonstick pan for this recipe; it can't achieve the heat level you need for excellent browning.

SERVES 4

FOR THE PARMESAN BUTTER

6 Tbsp (3 oz/90 g) unsalted butter, at room temperature, cut into chunks

½ cup (2 oz/60 g) freshly grated Parmesan cheese

Kosher salt and coarsely cracked pepper

4 filets mignons, each about ¾ lb (375 g) and 1½ inches (4 cm) thick, patted dry with paper towels

Olive oil

Kosher salt and freshly ground pepper

About 4 cups (4 oz/120 g) watercress, lightly dressed with Basic Vinaigrette (page 250)

1 Tbsp fresh thyme leaves

To make the Parmesan butter, in a mini food processor, combine the butter, cheese, ¼ teaspoon salt, and ¼ teaspoon pepper. Pulse until smooth. Set aside at room temperature. (At this point, the butter can be refrigerated in an airtight container for up to 2 weeks. Bring to room temperature before serving.)

Rub both sides of the steaks with olive oil. Let stand for 1 hour at room temperature.

Heat a large, ovenproof frying pan over high heat until very hot, about 3 minutes. Generously season both sides of the steaks with salt and pepper. Add enough olive oil to the pan to coat the bottom, and reduce the heat to medium-high. When the oil is shimmering, use tongs to place the steaks in the pan so they do not touch. Cook without moving for 2½ minutes. Turn the steaks and cook for 2 minutes more. Place the steaks on a rack set over a plate and let stand for at least 30 minutes or up to 1 hour. Set the pan aside.

Preheat the oven to 425°F (220°C). Return the steaks to the pan, place in the oven, and cook until an instant-read thermometer inserted into a steak registers 130°–135°F (54°–57°C) for medium-rare, 11–12 minutes, or until done to your liking. Place the steaks on the rack and let rest, uncovered, for 3–5 minutes.

Arrange the steaks on plates and top each with a large spoonful of Parmesan butter. Nestle the watercress alongside each steak, sprinkle with the thyme, and serve.

star of the show

Greatness doesn't need much adornment, so when you splurge on a special cut of meat, like filet mignon, keep the sides and the presentation simple.

Brined Pork Loin with Apricot-Onion Mostarda

This loin is made tender and juicy with an overnight brine. The leftovers make great sandwiches—smear a baguette with a little mayo or aioli and top with pork slices and a dollop of the mostarda.

SERVES 4–6

½ cup (4 oz/125 g) kosher salt

½ cup (3½ oz/105 g) firmly packed light brown sugar

1 Tbsp freshly ground pepper

1 yellow onion, finely chopped

5 cloves garlic, crushed

3 sprigs fresh thyme, plus 2 tsp chopped fresh thyme

3 sprigs fresh rosemary, plus 2 tsp chopped fresh rosemary

1 boneless center-cut pork loin, about 3 lb (1.5 kg), rolled and tied by the butcher

2 tsp olive oil

FOR THE MOSTARDA

1 Tbsp olive oil

1 yellow onion, thinly sliced

Pinch of kosher salt

¾ cup (4 oz/125 g) dried apricots (about 12), chopped

¼ cup (2 oz/60 g) sugar

¾ cup (6 fl oz/180 ml) dry white wine

2 Tbsp Dijon mustard

1 Tbsp white wine vinegar

In a large saucepan, combine the salt, brown sugar, pepper, onion, garlic, and herb sprigs. Pour in 3 cups (24 fl oz/ 750 ml) water and place over medium heat. Stir until the salt and sugar dissolve. Pour 6 cups (48 fl oz/1.5 l) cold water into a metal or glass dish large enough to hold the pork loin. Add the salt-sugar mixture and stir to combine. Let cool. Carefully submerge the pork loin in the brine, adding cold water, if needed, to submerge the pork in liquid. Cover and refrigerate for at least 3 hours or up to 24 hours.

Preheat the oven to 350°F (180°C). Remove the pork from the brine and pat dry with paper towels (discard the brine). Rub all over with the olive oil, then with the chopped herbs.

Place the pork in a roasting pan and roast for 30 minutes. Turn over and continue to roast until an instant-read thermometer inserted into the thickest part registers 140°F (60°C), about 20 minutes longer.

Meanwhile, make the mostarda: In a nonreactive frying pan over medium heat, warm the olive oil. Add the onion and salt and cook, stirring often, until the onion is beginning to caramelize, about 10 minutes. Add the apricots, sugar, wine, mustard, and vinegar and bring to a simmer. Reduce the heat to medium-low and simmer gently until the onion and apricots are tender and the sauce has thickened but is still somewhat syrupy, about 10 minutes. Remove the sauce from the heat and cover to keep warm.

Turn the pork again and raise the oven temperature to 450°F (230°C). Roast until the top is browned, about 5 minutes longer. Transfer the pork to a cutting board, tent with aluminum foil, and let rest for 10–15 minutes. Cut into slices and serve with the mostarda.

Pork Chops with Caramelized Meyer Lemons

Here, thinly sliced Meyer lemons, which are at their peak from late fall to early spring, add brightness to pan-seared pork chops and make a beautiful, fresh presentation for a small gathering. Seek out good pork from heritage producers for the best flavor.

SERVES 4

2 Tbsp olive oil

3 cloves garlic, very thinly sliced

4 fresh bay leaves, or 6 dried bay leaves

2 Meyer lemons, 1 thinly sliced and 1 halved

4 bone-in, center-cut pork chops, each 6–8 oz (185–250 g)

Salt and freshly ground pepper

In a large cast-iron or other heavy-bottomed frying pan over medium heat, warm the olive oil, garlic, and bay leaves. Sauté until the garlic is lightly golden and the olive oil is infused with the aroma of garlic and bay leaf, about 5 minutes. Transfer the garlic and bay leaves to a plate and set aside. Add the lemon slices to the pan and cook, turning once, until lightly browned, about 2 minutes per side. Transfer to the plate with the garlic and bay leaves.

Season the pork chops with salt and pepper. Arrange in the pan and raise the heat to medium-high. Sear until nicely browned on the bottoms, 2–3 minutes. Turn the chops and cook until browned on the second sides, 2–3 minutes longer. Squeeze the lemon halves over the chops and turn to coat them with the juice. Return the garlic, bay leaves, and lemon slices to the pan and reduce the heat to medium-low. Cook until the chops spring back but still feel tender if gently pressed with a finger and the centers are very slightly pink when cut into with a knife, 3–4 minutes longer.

Place the pork chops on a serving platter, spoon the pan juices and the lemon slices over the top, and serve.

asian comfort food

Crispy Shallots and Chiles (page 196)
lend extra flavor and crispy texture
to this fragrant pork dish.

Braised Spiced Pork with Rice Noodles & Bok Choy

Braising the pork with soy sauce and spices, the Chinese technique called red cooking, results in meat that is meltingly tender and creates a rich broth perfect for ladling over noodles. If enoki mushrooms are not available, bean sprouts and cilantro can take their place.

SERVES 6

FOR THE MARINADE

2 lemongrass stalks, tough outer layers removed, stalks lightly smashed and finely chopped

2 shallots, finely chopped

2 Tbsp soy sauce, preferably low-sodium

1 Tbsp fish sauce

1 Tbsp sambal oelek

1 Tbsp firmly packed light brown sugar

1 tsp Chinese five-spice powder

1 boneless pork shoulder (Boston butt), about 2 lb (1 kg), tied and halved crosswise

2 Tbsp canola oil

3 cups (24 fl oz/750 ml) chicken broth, preferably fat-free and low-sodium

6 small baby bok choy

1 lb (500 g) round or wide fresh rice noodles

1 package (3½ oz/100 g) enoki mushrooms, tough bottoms removed

6 strips orange zest, each 1 by 2 inches (2.5 by 5 cm), thinly cut lengthwise

6 fresh mint sprigs

To make the marinade, in a large bowl, combine the lemongrass, shallots, soy sauce, fish sauce, sambal oelek, brown sugar, and five-spice powder.

Add the pork to the bowl and rub with the marinade. Cover and refrigerate at least 4 hours or up to 24 hours. Remove the pork from the marinade, scraping any bits clinging to the meat back into the bowl. Reserve the marinade.

In a large, heavy pot over medium-high heat, warm the oil. Add the pork and brown on all sides, about 10 minutes. Pour in the reserved marinade and the broth. When the liquid starts to simmer, cover partially and cook until the meat is tender, about 1½ hours, turning it 3 or 4 times. Remove from the heat and let the meat cool in the liquid.

Cut the meat into 6 slices. Pour the braising liquid into a small metal bowl, let stand for a few minutes, then skim the fat from the surface with a large spoon. Set aside.

Bring a large pot of water to a boil. Ready a bowl of ice water. Plunge the bok choy into the boiling water just until bright green, about 30 seconds. Using tongs, transfer them to the ice water. Drain well and set aside. Add the noodles to the boiling water and cook according to the package directions. Drain, rinse briefly with cold water, then divide among 6 warmed wide, shallow bowls and set briefly aside.

In a deep frying pan over medium-high heat, warm the pork and braising liquid until the liquid simmers. Add the bok choy for a few seconds to rewarm them, then transfer a bok choy and a slice of pork to each bowl of noodles. Pour the braising liquid over each bowl, dividing it evenly. Divide the enoki among the bowls, sprinkle with orange zest, garnish with the mint sprigs, and serve.

Stir-Fried Shrimp with Asparagus, Lemongrass & Mint

This easy stir-fry is all about the bright flavors of springtime—asparagus, citrusy lemongrass, and refreshing mint. Sweet, briny shrimp are perfect candidates for a stir-fry because they can be marinated and cooked quickly. The same mix of ingredients is also good with scallops or sliced chicken breast.

SERVES 6

1½ lb (750 g) shrimp, peeled and deveined

3 cloves garlic, minced

2 Tbsp peeled and minced fresh ginger

¼ cup (2 fl oz/60 ml) canola oil

Salt

½ cup (4 fl oz/125 ml) soy sauce

6 Tbsp (3 fl oz/90 ml) rice vinegar

6 Tbsp (3 fl oz/90 ml) white wine

3 Tbsp honey

1 Tbsp cornstarch

1 Tbsp Asian sesame oil

½ cup minced shallots

6-inch (15-cm) piece lemongrass base, outer leaves removed, thinly sliced

1½ red bell peppers, seeded and cut into strips 1 inch (2.5 cm) wide

1 bunch asparagus, tough ends removed, cut into 1-inch (2.5-cm) pieces

Jasmine rice (page 249) for serving

3 Tbsp chopped fresh mint

In a bowl, toss the shrimp, garlic, ginger, 1½ tablespoons of the canola oil, and a pinch of salt. Let marinate for 30 minutes.

In a small bowl, combine the soy sauce, vinegar, wine, honey, cornstarch, and sesame oil and stir until the cornstarch dissolves. Set aside.

In a wok or deep frying pan over high heat, warm 1½ tablespoons of the canola oil. Add the shrimp with the marinade and stir-fry until almost cooked through, about 2 minutes. Transfer to a bowl and keep warm.

Add the remaining 1 tablespoon oil to the wok and heat until hot. Add the shallots and lemongrass and stir-fry until fragrant, about 1 minute. Add the bell pepper and asparagus and stir-fry until tender-crisp, about 2 minutes.

Return the shrimp to the wok, add the soy sauce mixture, and stir-fry until everything is piping hot and the sauce has thickened slightly, about 2 minutes.

Divide the rice among 6 bowls, top with the stir-fry, sprinkle with the mint, and serve.

Whole-Roasted Fish Stuffed with Fennel & Thyme

This is a good choice for entertaining because it's easy to prepare and can be made ahead. Stuff the fish a few hours ahead, place on a baking sheet, and refrigerate, then pop in the oven about 20 minutes before serving time. Serve with wilted spinach and small red potatoes dressed with butter and parsley, and pour a well-chilled French Chablis.

SERVES 6

2 fennel bulbs, fronds reserved, bulbs thinly sliced crosswise, preferably with a mandoline

2 Tbsp chopped fresh thyme

Salt and freshly ground pepper

Pinch of red pepper flakes

3 sea bass, 1½–2 lb (750 g–1 kg) total, cleaned

Olive oil for drizzling

Lemon wedges

Preheat the oven to 500°F (260°C).

Coarsely chop the fennel fronds to measure about ¼ cup (1 oz/30 g). In a bowl, toss together the sliced fennel bulbs, half of the chopped fronds, and the thyme. Season with salt, pepper, and red pepper flakes and mix well.

Make 3 diagonal slices about ½ inch (12 mm) deep on both sides of each fish. Season all sides with salt and pepper. Stuff the cavities with the fennel mixture and secure with toothpicks. Scatter the remaining fennel fronds on a heavy rimmed baking sheet, place the fish on top, and drizzle with olive oil. Roast the fish until the flesh flakes easily when lightly pressed, about 15 minutes.

Transfer the fish to a platter along with juices from the pan. Discard the fennel fronds on the baking sheet. Remove the toothpicks. Serve the fish with the lemon wedges.

Roasted Halibut Steaks with Nectarine Chutney

Everything is cooked in one pan in this easy summertime dish, making it a terrific option for entertaining. The nectarines are baked to become a fragrant chutney and the fish is roasted on top.

SERVES 4

5 ripe nectarines, halved, pitted, and cut into wedges

1 Tbsp olive oil, plus more for brushing

2 Tbsp minced red onion

1 tsp fresh lemon juice

1 tsp light brown sugar

1 tsp peeled and grated fresh ginger

4 halibut fillets, about 5 oz (155 g) each

Salt and freshly ground pepper

Fresh tarragon leaves for garnish (optional)

Preheat the oven to 400°F (200°C).

In a baking dish, combine the nectarines, olive oil, onion, lemon juice, brown sugar, and ginger. Stir to coat, then spread evenly in the dish.

Brush the fillets with olive oil, then season on both sides with salt and pepper. Place the fillets on top of the nectarine mixture and roast until the fish is opaque throughout and flakes easily with a fork and the fruit is tender, 15–20 minutes.

To serve, use a spatula to transfer a fillet to each of 4 warmed individual plates, top each with a spoonful of chutney, and sprinkle with tarragon leaves, if using. Serve, passing the remaining chutney at the table.

summertime sips

Pair this dish with an herbal Sauvignon
Blanc or a good white Bordeaux.

Pappardelle with Sausage & Fennel Ragù

Endless renditions of ragù, a thick meat sauce, are made throughout Italy. This chunky version is especially tasty because of the pairing of fennel and pork. Pappardelle is ideal for supporting the hearty sauce, but bucatini and short-cut pastas will work well, too.

SERVES 4–6

1 fennel bulb

4 Tbsp (2 fl oz/60 ml) olive oil

1 lb (500 g) sweet Italian sausages, casings removed

1 large red onion, chopped

2 large cloves garlic, chopped

½ tsp ground fennel seeds

1 cup (8 fl oz/250 ml) dry red wine

3 Tbsp tomato paste

Big pinch of saffron threads soaked in 1 Tbsp hot chicken broth, or ⅛ tsp powdered saffron

1½ cups (9 oz/280 g) drained canned crushed tomatoes

1 tsp minced fresh marjoram, or ½ tsp crumbled dried marjoram

1½ cups (12 fl oz/375 ml) chicken broth, preferably low-sodium, plus more as needed

Salt and freshly ground pepper

1 lb (500 g) pappardelle

Freshly grated Parmesan cheese for serving

Cut off the stems and feathery tops from the fennel bulb and remove any bruised outer stalks. Slice off and discard the tough bottom of the bulb, then quarter the bulb lengthwise. Core and finely chop the bulb.

In a Dutch oven or large, deep frying pan over medium heat, warm 2 tablespoons of the olive oil. Add the sausage and cook until lightly browned but still pink inside, about 5 minutes. Use a wooden spoon to break up the sausage as it cooks, but keep the texture chunky. Using a slotted spoon, place the sausage on a plate and set aside. Drain off the excess fat from the pan.

Add the remaining 2 tablespoons olive oil to the pan and warm over medium heat. Add the chopped fennel bulb, onion, garlic, and ground fennel seeds and sauté until all the vegetables are softened, about 8 minutes. Return the sausage to the pan and stir in the wine and tomato paste. Sauté until most of the wine has evaporated, about 3 minutes. Add the saffron with its soaking broth, the tomatoes, and the marjoram and simmer for 5 minutes. Add the chicken broth and simmer gently, uncovered, until the sauce becomes aromatic and the flavors are blended, about 45 minutes. Add more broth if the sauce begins to dry out. Season to taste with salt and pepper. Reduce the heat to low and cover the pan to keep the sauce warm.

Bring a large pot of salted water to a boil. Add the pasta and cook, stirring occasionally, until al dente, according to the package directions.

Drain the pasta and transfer to a warmed serving bowl. Add the sauce and toss until well combined. Serve with the cheese to pass at the table.

Butternut Squash Risotto with Sage

Sweet butternut squash has an affinity for sage, whether in soups, in pasta dishes, or simply roasted and tossed. This basic Parmesan risotto is the perfect means to highlight the flavors of shredded squash and sage leaves, which are stirred directly into the creamy rice.

SERVES 4–6

2–3 cloves garlic, chopped

Salt and freshly ground pepper

1 small butternut squash, about 1 lb (500 g)

4 cups (32 fl oz/1 l) vegetable or chicken broth

4 Tbsp (2 oz/60 g) unsalted butter

2 Tbsp olive oil

1 yellow onion, chopped

1½ cups (10½ oz/330 g) Arborio or Carnaroli rice

5 fresh sage leaves, finely shredded

1½ cups (12 fl oz/375 ml) dry white wine

Pinch of freshly grated nutmeg

1 cup (4 oz/125 g) freshly grated Parmesan cheese

In a small bowl, using a fork, crush the garlic with a pinch of salt. Peel the squash, halve it, and scoop out the seeds and fibers. Cut one squash half into ½-inch (12-mm) cubes and coarsely shred the remaining half.

In a saucepan, bring the broth to a gentle simmer over medium heat and maintain over low heat.

In a large, heavy saucepan, melt 2 tablespoons of the butter with the oil over medium heat. Add the cubed squash and the onion and sauté until softened, 5–7 minutes. Raise the heat to medium-high, add the rice, and cook, stirring, until well coated with the butter and oil and semi-translucent, 3–5 minutes. Add the sage and pour in ¾ cup (6 fl oz/180 ml) of the wine. Cook, stirring, until the wine is absorbed. Stir in the remaining wine and cook and stir until absorbed. Add the simmering broth a ladleful at a time, stirring until almost all the broth is absorbed before adding more broth. When the rice is almost tender, after about 15 minutes, stir in the shredded squash. Continue to cook, adding more broth as needed and stirring constantly, until the rice is firm but tender, 20–25 minutes longer. Stir in the garlic and the nutmeg and season with salt and pepper. Add additional hot broth if needed. Stir in ½ cup (2 oz/60 g) of the Parmesan cheese. Spoon the risotto into bowls. Cut the remaining 2 tablespoons butter into pieces, and top each serving with a piece of butter. Serve with the remaining cheese to pass at the table.

selecting dried pasta

When building a meal around dried pasta, look for an Italian brand. Even products made by big commercial companies typically have a better taste and texture than those made elsewhere. Experiment with artisanal brands as well, and feel free to mix and match sauces to different pasta shapes to find favorite combinations.

Bucatini with Pancetta & Caramelized Onions

Sweet caramelized onions and salty pancetta are combined in this rustic dish that's easy to make for weeknight entertaining. Perciatelli or even spaghetti can be substituted for the bucatini. Uncork a Trebbiano or other soft Italian white to balance the earthiness of the pasta.

SERVES 4

½ lb (250 g) pancetta, cut into ¼-inch (6-mm) dice

4 Tbsp olive oil

8 oz (250 g) mixed mushrooms (such as morels, porcini, shiitake, or cremini), halved if large

2½ lb (1.25 kg) red onions, yellow onions, or a mix, halved and very thinly sliced lengthwise

2 tsp minced fresh oregano

Salt and freshly ground pepper

1 lb (500 g) bucatini

½ cup (4 fl oz/125 ml) dry white wine

½ cup (2 oz/60 g) freshly grated pecorino romano cheese, plus more for serving

In a large sauté pan over medium-low heat, sauté the pancetta until lightly crisped and a little of the fat is rendered, about 10 minutes. Using a slotted spoon, transfer to paper towels to drain.

In the same pan over medium heat, warm 2 tablespoons of the olive oil. Add the mushrooms and cook, stirring occasionally, until tender and lightly browned, about 5 minutes. Using a slotted spoon, transfer the mushrooms to a plate.

Add the remaining 2 tablespoons olive oil to the pan. Add the onions and stir until evenly coated with the oil. Cover and cook over medium-low heat until the onions are well softened, 15–20 minutes. Add the oregano, 1 teaspoon salt, and a generous grinding of pepper and cook, uncovered, until golden brown, creamy, and greatly reduced in volume, about 30 minutes longer. Stir from time to time to prevent scorching.

Meanwhile, bring a large pot of salted water to a boil. Add the bucatini, stir, and cook, stirring occasionally, until al dente, according to the package directions. Drain, reserving about ½ cup (4 fl oz/125 ml) of the cooking water.

Raise the heat under the onions to medium-high, pour in the wine, and stir to scrape up any browned bits from the pan bottom. Let simmer for a minute, then add the reserved pancetta and mushrooms with any accumulated juices. Transfer the pasta to the pan and toss gently to combine. Add one or two spoonfuls of the pasta cooking water to loosen the sauce, if needed. Sprinkle with the cheese and toss to combine. Divide among 4 shallow bowls and serve, passing additional cheese at the table.

Fresh Tomato, Basil & Fontina Pizza

With the dough and tomato sauce on hand, you can get this hearty vegetarian pizza on the table in less time than it takes for a delivery from your local pizzeria. If you don't have a pizza stone, a baking sheet will do; just bake on the lowest rack to ensure a crisp crust.

SERVES 4

Pizza Dough (page 248) or 1 lb (500 g) purchased pizza dough

1 cup (8 fl oz/250 ml) Quick Pizza Sauce (page 249) or purchased pizza sauce

1 cup (4 oz/125 g) shredded fontina cheese

½ cup (2 oz/65 g) shredded mozzarella cheese

½ cup (3 oz/90 g) mix of red, yellow, and orange cherry tomatoes, halved

2 ripe plum tomatoes, sliced

Olive oil for brushing

Salt and freshly ground pepper

Basil leaves for garnish

variations

Switch it up according to what's in season and personal preference. Try these inspired topping combinations:

• Grilled peaches, prosciutto, mozzarella, and fresh arugula to finish

• Shaved Brussels sprouts, bacon, red onion, balsamic drizzle, mozzarella

• Kale, chicken, roasted garlic, smoked cheddar

• Spicy kalamata olives, anchovies, capers, tomato sauce, mozzarella

• Shaved asparagus, red pepper pesto, baked egg, goat cheese

• Roasted squash, fried sage, smoked mozzarella, caramelized onion

• Sautéed leeks, shaved red-skinned potatoes, rosemary, béchamel sauce

Place a pizza stone in the middle of the oven and preheat to 450°F (230°C). Once the oven has reached 450°F (230°C), let the stone continue to heat for 15–30 minutes longer, without opening the door.

On a floured pizza peel, stretch or roll out the pizza dough into a 12-inch (30-cm) round. If the dough springs back, let it rest for about 10 minutes before continuing. Leaving a 1-inch (2.5-cm) border, spread the sauce over the dough round and top with the cheese. Arrange the tomato halves and slices on top. Brush the outside edge of the dough with olive oil. Season the pizza lightly with salt and pepper.

Carefully slide the pizza from the peel onto the hot stone in the oven and bake for 10–12 minutes, or until the crust is golden brown. Using the peel, transfer the pizza to a cutting board. Let cool for a few minutes, garnish with basil leaves, then slice and serve right away.

Barley Pilaf with Chanterelles

Flavorful pearl barley replaces the usual rice in this quick and easy pilaf. Chanterelles are called for here, but other seasonal wild or cultivated mushrooms can be used as well, such as porcini, morels, shiitakes, or oyster mushrooms.

SERVES 8–10

4 Tbsp (2 oz/60 g) unsalted butter

1 leek, including tender green top, finely chopped

½ lb (250 g) fresh chanterelle mushrooms, sliced lengthwise

2 Tbsp finely chopped fresh thyme leaves

2½ cups (17½ oz/545 g) quick-cooking pearl barley

1 cup (8 fl oz/250 ml) dry white wine

2½ cups (20 fl oz/625 ml) chicken broth, preferably low-sodium, heated

Coarse sea salt and freshly ground pepper

In a large saucepan over medium heat, melt the butter. Add the leek and sauté until translucent, about 4 minutes. Raise the heat to medium-high, add the chanterelles, and cook, stirring, until soft, about 3 minutes.

Add the thyme and barley and stir to coat with the butter. Pour in the wine and cook until absorbed, about 1 minute. Add the broth and bring to a boil, then reduce the heat to low, cover, and cook until the liquid has been absorbed and the barley is tender, about 13 minutes. Remove from the heat and let stand for 5 minutes to allow the flavors to blend.

Season to taste with salt and pepper, transfer to a warmed serving bowl, and serve.

Oven-Roasted Ratatouille

Traditionally, ratatouille is a dish of summer vegetables that are simmered for a long time in their own juices. In this version, the vegetables are cut into large pieces and roasted briefly, which concentrates and intensifies their flavors.

SERVES 6–8

1 lb (500 g) plum tomatoes, halved lengthwise

4 large cloves garlic, sliced

1 large yellow onion, halved and cut crosswise into slices ¼ inch (6 mm) thick

1 small eggplant, trimmed and cut into 1-inch (2.5-cm) chunks

1 small zucchini, trimmed and cut crosswise into slices ½ inch (12 mm) thick

1 small yellow crookneck squash, trimmed and cut crosswise into slices ½ inch (12 mm) thick

1 green bell pepper, seeded and cut into 1½-inch (4-cm) squares

5 Tbsp (3 fl oz/80 ml) olive oil

Salt and freshly ground pepper

¼ cup (⅓ oz/10 g) finely shredded fresh basil

2 Tbsp chopped fresh thyme

Preheat the oven to 425°F (220°C).

In a large bowl, combine the tomatoes, garlic, onion, eggplant, zucchini, yellow squash, and bell pepper. Drizzle in the olive oil, sprinkle generously with salt, and toss to coat. Transfer the vegetables to a large rimmed baking sheet and arrange in a single layer.

Roast the vegetables, stirring once or twice, for 20 minutes. Remove from the oven and sprinkle with the basil and thyme. Continue to roast, again stirring once or twice, until the biggest pieces are tender when pierced with a fork, 5–10 minutes longer. Remove the vegetables from the oven and season with salt and pepper.

Transfer the ratatouille to a bowl. Serve hot, warm, or at room temperature.

Asparagus with Parmesan Bread Crumbs

Here's a wonderful way to serve asparagus, which is at its best in the spring. The tender stalks are tossed with olive oil, then topped with a savory mixture of bread crumbs, parsley, lemon zest, and Parmesan cheese before roasting.

SERVES 6

1½ lb (750 g) asparagus, tough ends removed

3 Tbsp olive oil

1½ cups (6 oz/180 g) grated Parmesan cheese

¼ cup (1 oz/30 g) dried bread crumbs

1½ Tbsp minced fresh flat-leaf parsley

1½ Tbsp grated lemon zest

3 Tbsp fresh lemon juice

Salt and freshly ground pepper

Preheat the oven to 450°F (230°C).

Place the asparagus in a baking dish and drizzle with 1½ tablespoons of the olive oil. Toss the spears gently to coat and arrange in a single layer.

In a bowl, stir together the cheese, bread crumbs, parsley, and lemon zest with 1½ tablespoons of the lemon juice, 1 teaspoon salt, and a liberal grinding of pepper. Drizzle in the remaining 1½ tablespoons olive oil and stir until mixed. Sprinkle the bread-crumb mixture over the asparagus and roast, uncovered, until the asparagus is just tender and the topping is golden brown, 15 minutes.

Drizzle the asparagus with the remaining 1½ tablespoons lemon juice and serve.

Coconut-Curry Butternut Squash Soup

At once fragrant, sweet, and spicy, this soup is spiked with unexpected Thai flavors. The butternut squash will give the immune system a powerful beta-carotene boost. Garnish it with Thai purple basil leaves and blossoms, if you like.

SERVES 4–6

1 large butternut squash (about 4 lb/2 kg)

1½ Tbsp olive oil

4 large shallots (about 3 oz/90 g), sliced

1 Tbsp peeled and grated fresh ginger

1 clove garlic, minced

3 cups (24 fl oz/750 ml) chicken or vegetable broth, preferably low-sodium, plus more as needed

Salt

1 tsp Thai red curry paste

¾ cup (6 fl oz/180 ml) light coconut milk

2 tsp fresh lime juice

Using a sharp, heavy knife, trim the stem end from the squash, then cut lengthwise into halves. Scoop out the seeds and discard. Peel and then cut the flesh into 1-inch (2.5-cm) cubes (about 9 cups/3 lb/1.5 kg).

In a soup pot over medium heat, warm the olive oil. Add the shallots and cook until softened, 2–3 minutes. Add the ginger and garlic and cook until fragrant but not browned, about 1 minute. Add the squash, broth, and ½ teaspoon salt and bring to a boil over high heat. Reduce the heat to medium-low, cover, and simmer until the squash is tender when pierced with a fork, about 20 minutes. Remove from the heat and let cool slightly.

In a small bowl, combine the curry paste and coconut milk and whisk until well blended. Set aside.

In a blender or food processor, working in batches if necessary, process the soup until smooth. Return the soup to the pot and stir in the coconut milk mixture. Stir in more broth if needed. Reheat the soup gently over medium heat just until hot. Season with lime juice and salt to taste. Ladle into warmed individual bowls and serve.

Cauliflower Soup with Crispy Prosciutto

Be careful not to over salt the soup, as the prosciutto garnish will add a good amount of salt. To make this dish vegetarian, use vegetable broth in place of the chicken broth and substitute crispy fried shallots (page 196) for the prosciutto.

SERVES 4–6

2 oz (60 g) thinly sliced prosciutto

2 Tbsp unsalted butter

1 yellow onion, chopped

2 ribs celery, chopped

2 cloves garlic, minced

1 head cauliflower, coarsely chopped (about 4 cups)

¼ tsp freshly grated nutmeg

4 cups (32 fl oz/1 l) chicken broth, plus more as needed

¼ cup (2 fl oz/60 ml) heavy cream

Salt and ground white pepper

Preheat the oven to 375°F (190°C). Place the prosciutto slices in a single layer on a baking sheet. Bake until crispy, 15–18 minutes. Let cool, then crumble and set aside.

In a large, heavy pot over medium-high heat, melt the butter. Add the onion, celery, and garlic and sauté until soft, 5–7 minutes. Add the cauliflower and nutmeg, stir well to coat, and cook for 5 minutes. Add the broth and bring to a boil. Reduce the heat to low and simmer until the cauliflower is very tender, 20–25 minutes. Remove from the heat and let cool slightly.

Working in batches if necessary, purée the soup in a blender. Return to the pot and, if needed, add more broth to thin the soup. Stir in the cream. Return the soup just to a boil and season to taste with salt and white pepper. Ladle the soup into warmed individual bowls, garnish with the prosciutto, and serve.

Roasted Tomatoes with Fresh Herbs

Roasting intensifies the flavor of tomatoes, and these are fantastic with roast meats or sautéed fish or in sandwiches or salads. Chilled, drizzled with olive oil and balsamic vinegar, and paired with Fontina, they make an elegant starter. They can also be puréed and used as a tasty sauce on pizza or pasta.

SERVES 6

2 Tbsp olive oil, plus more for greasing

2 lb (1 kg) assorted tomatoes, halved if large

2 cloves garlic, pressed

1 Tbsp minced fresh oregano leaves

2 tsp minced fresh thyme leaves

¼ tsp salt

Preheat the oven to 375°F (190°C). Brush a large, heavy rimmed baking sheet or other baking pan with olive oil. In a bowl, toss together the tomatoes, oil, garlic, oregano, and thyme. Arrange the tomatoes, cut sides up, on the prepared baking pan. Sprinkle the tomatoes with the salt. Roast the tomatoes until they are soft and beginning to brown, about 50 minutes. Let the tomatoes cool to room temperature on the baking sheet. Serve at room temperature.

summer hues

July and August bring a dazzling array of tomato choices to farmers' markets, from tiny, sweet cherry or grape varieties to heirlooms in shades of yellow, green, pink, red, and more. Take advantage of the bounty and use contrasting colors and shapes in dishes that call for these menu favorites.

Honey-Balsamic Roasted Carrots

While the honey heightens the natural sweetness of the carrots, the balsamic tempers the overall sugar of this simple yet handsome vegetable side. To lessen last-minute work, peel the carrots and immerse them in cold water early in the day, so they are ready to roast at dinnertime.

SERVES 6

2 bunches baby carrots, about 2 lb (1 kg) total weight, trimmed and peeled

1 Tbsp olive oil

4 sprigs fresh thyme

Salt and freshly ground pepper

2 Tbsp balsamic vinegar

2 Tbsp honey

Preheat the oven to 425°F (220°C).

In a shallow baking dish, toss the carrots with the olive oil and thyme sprigs and season with salt and pepper. Roast for 15 minutes.

In a small bowl, whisk together the vinegar and honey. Drizzle over the carrots and shake the baking dish a few times to coat. Roast, shaking the dish once or twice, until the carrots are tender and caramelized, about 15 minutes longer.

Spicy Broccolini with Garlic

Assertive seasonings like garlic and red pepper flakes complement the sweet, grassy flavor of broccolini in this simple side, ideal for serving with roasted, sautéed, or grilled meats. If you cannot find broccolini in the market, use broccoli in its place, cutting the whole head—stalk and crown—lengthwise into slender spears.

SERVES 4–6

1½ lb (750 g) broccolini, trimmed

¼ cup (2 fl oz/60 ml) olive oil

3 Tbsp fresh lemon juice, plus more for serving

3 cloves garlic, minced

Pinch of red pepper flakes

Salt

Preheat the oven to 400°F (200°C).

Using a vegetable peeler or a sharp paring knife, peel off any dried or bruised skin from the broccolini stems. Cut any large florets lengthwise, so all are about the same size. Place the broccolini in a medium bowl. Pour olive oil over the broccolini, sprinkle with the lemon juice, garlic, and red pepper flakes, and toss to coat thoroughly. Arrange the broccolini in a single layer in a pan. Roast, turning once, until the broccolini is tender and the tips and outer edges are crisp and browned, about 15 minutes. Serve with a drizzle of lemon juice and a few pinches of salt.

Fruit Desserts Four Ways

figs + balsamic vinegar

2 Tbsp wildflower honey or other full-flavored honey
1 Tbsp unsalted butter • 1 Tbsp aged balsamic vinegar
½ tsp peppercorns, lightly crushed • Salt • 12 ripe fresh
Mission or Calimyrna figs • Small fresh mint sprigs for garnish
Mascarpone or vanilla ice cream for serving (optional)

Preheat the oven to 425°F (220°C). In a small saucepan over medium-low heat, combine the honey, butter, vinegar, peppercorns, and a pinch of salt. Warm until the mixture loosens into a sauce, about 5 minutes.

Lightly grease a 10-inch (25-cm) baking dish. Cut each fig lengthwise through the stem into quarters, stopping just short of the bottoms so the quarters are still attached. Carefully arrange the figs standing upright in the prepared pan and nudge the cut ends open like flower petals. Spoon the sauce over the figs.

Bake until the figs are softened and lightly caramelized, 10–15 minutes. Arrange the figs on a serving platter and drizzle with the sauce from the baking dish. Garnish with mint sprigs. Serve warm with mascarpone or vanilla ice cream, if you like.

SERVES 4–6

pears + honey

⅓ cup (4½ fl oz/140 ml) honey • 4 bay leaves • 3 Tbsp unsalted butter, cut into 6 pieces • 3 ripe but firm Bosc pears, peeled, halved, and cored • 2 Tbsp amaretto liqueur • ⅓ cup (1½ oz/45 g) slivered almonds, toasted • 1½ cups (12 oz/375 g) plain Greek yogurt, whisked until smooth

Preheat the oven to 375°F (190°C). In a Dutch oven or heavy ovenproof sauté pan over medium-high heat, combine the honey and bay leaves and bring to a simmer. Reduce the heat to medium and simmer, stirring occasionally, until the honey turns a rich amber color, about 3 minutes. Remove from the heat. Place the butter pieces on the honey, spacing them evenly. Using tongs, carefully place a pear half, cut side down, on top of each piece of butter. Cover the pot and roast in the oven for 10 minutes. Turn the pears over and baste with the honey mixture. Drizzle with the amaretto and continue to roast, uncovered, until tender, 6–8 minutes longer. Remove from the oven and let the pears cool slightly in the honey mixture.

Arrange the pears on a platter and drizzle with the honey mixture from the pan. Sprinkle with the almonds. Serve with the yogurt.

SERVES 6

These simple fruit desserts are delicious proof that the most memorable conclusion to any meal often requires nothing more than great ingredients and a bit of ingenuity.

raspberries + lemongrass

1 stalk lemongrass • ⅓ cup (3 oz/90 g) sugar
4 pt (2 lb/1 kg) raspberries • Sweetened whipped cream
Sprig of fresh currants for garnish (optional)

Remove the dry outer leaves from the base of the lemongrass stalk and trim off the grassy tops, leaving the 3-inch (7.5-cm) base. Trim the roots from the base. Using the back of the blade of a chef's knife, bruise the lemongrass, flattening the stalk and breaking some of the fibers to release its aroma.

In a small saucepan over medium-high heat, combine the sugar and ⅓ cup (3 fl oz/80 ml) water and bring to a simmer, swirling occasionally, until the sugar is dissolved, about 2 minutes. Remove from the heat. Add the lemongrass, cover, and let cool for 30 minutes. Strain the lemongrass syrup through a sieve into a large bowl, pressing on the stalk with the back of a spoon to extract as much syrup as possible. Discard the lemongrass.

Add the raspberries to the syrup and stir gently. Divide the raspberries and syrup among individual bowls. Top with a dollop of whipped cream, garnish with currants, if using, and serve.

SERVES 4–6

plums + star anise

8 ripe black plums, halved and pitted • 1 Tbsp firmly
packed light brown sugar • 8 star anise pods
Vanilla frozen yogurt or Vanilla Whipped Cream (page 250)

Preheat the oven to 400°F (200°C). Lightly grease a baking dish just large enough to hold the plum halves in a single layer. Arrange the plums, cut side up, in the prepared dish. Sprinkle brown sugar over each plum half, dividing it evenly, then sprinkle the star anise pods over the top. Roast until the sugar has melted, the plums are warmed through, and the skins are just beginning to wrinkle a bit on the edges, about 15 minutes. Arrange the plums on a platter and let cool to warm, or serve hot. Serve with frozen yogurt.

SERVES 8

make it modern

Fresh figs and cherries make an
unexpected combination in this classic
Italian tart. Substitute them with any of
your favorite fresh stone fruits in season.

Almond Tart with Fresh Figs & Cherries

Put this elegant almond-rich tart on the menu of your next dinner party. To save time on party day, bake the tart shell up to two days in advance and store in an airtight container at room temperature, then make the filling and bake the tart early on the day of serving.

SERVES 8

Tart Pastry (page 248)

8 Tbsp (4 oz/125 g) unsalted butter, at room temperature

½ lb (250 g) almond paste, cut into pieces

¼ cup (2 oz/60 g) sugar

2 large eggs

⅓ cup (2 oz/60 g) all-purpose flour

6–8 ripe figs, stemmed and cut lengthwise into 4 slices

8–10 fresh cherries, stemmed and pitted

2 Tbsp honey, warmed

½ cup (2 oz/60 g) slice blanched almonds, toasted

Preheat the oven to 375°F (190°C). Prepare the tart pastry, cover, and refrigerate for at least 30 minutes. On a lightly floured work surface, roll out the dough into a round about 12 inches (33 cm) in diameter. Fold the dough round in half and carefully place it in a 9½-inch (24-cm) tart pan with a removable bottom. Unfold and ease the round into the pan, patting it firmly into the pan. Using kitchen scissors, trim the edge of the pastry, leaving about ½ inch (12 mm) extended over the pan rim. Fold the pastry edge inside the pan rim and press gently to extend the dough edge slightly above the rim to offset any shrinkage during baking. Refrigerate until firm, at least 30 minutes.

Prick the pastry shell at even intervals with the tines of a fork. Bake until dry and just beginning to color, about 25 minutes, checking the pastry shell halfway through baking to pop any air bubbles with the fork, as needed. Let cool.

Position a rack in the middle of the oven and reduce the heat to 350°F (180°C). In a bowl, using an electric mixer on medium speed or a whisk, beat the butter until smooth. Gradually add the almond paste, beating until smooth after each addition. Beat in the sugar. Add the eggs one at a time, beating well after each addition. Stir in the flour.

Spread the almond paste mixture evenly over the tart shell. Bake until just golden and the edges are set but the center still jiggles slightly, about 20 minutes.

Arrange the figs and cherries decoratively over the filling. Bake until golden and the center of the tart is firm, 20–25 minutes longer, checking the tart halfway through baking and covering the top loosely with aluminum foil if the filling begins to brown too quickly. Remove from the oven and immediately brush with the honey. Sprinkle with the almonds and let cool. Cut into wedges and serve.

Caramel
Pots de Crèmes

This smooth, creamy custard dessert flavored with caramel is one of the sweet comfort foods that people crave during cooler months. Garnish each serving with a dollop of whipped cream and toasted walnuts or pecans for an elegant presentation.

SERVES 6

1 cup (8 oz/250 g) sugar

1½ cups (12 fl oz/375 ml) heavy cream

1½ cups (12 fl oz/375 ml) whole milk

8 large egg yolks

Boiling water, for water bath

In a heavy saucepan over medium-high heat, combine the sugar and ⅓ cup (3 fl oz/80 ml) water, cover, and bring to a boil. Uncover and cook until the sugar turns golden amber in color, 8–12 minutes. Be careful, because the caramel is very hot.

Meanwhile, in a large saucepan over medium-high heat, combine the cream and milk and warm until small bubbles appear along the edges of the pan. Remove from the heat.

Preheat the oven to 325°F (165°C).

When the caramel is ready, add ¼ cup (2 fl oz/60 ml) water and whisk vigorously until the bubbles subside. Pour the caramel into the hot cream mixture and whisk together until mixed. Let cool for about 10 minutes.

In a bowl, whisk together the egg yolks. Slowly add the caramel-cream mixture to the egg yolks, stirring constantly with a wooden spoon until mixed. Strain through a fine-mesh sieve into a pitcher.

Pour the custard into six ⅔-cup (5–fl oz/160-ml) ramekins. Place the ramekins in a baking pan. Pour boiling water into the pan to reach about 1 inch (2.5 cm) up the sides of the ramekins. Bake until the edges of the custards are set, 40–50 minutes. Remove the baking pan from the oven and transfer to a rack to cool for 10 minutes.

Remove the custards from the water bath and let cool. Refrigerate for several hours or overnight until well chilled. Serve chilled or at room temperature.

Beignets with Dark Chocolate Sauce

A deep-fried pastry brought to New Orleans by French colonists, the classic morning pastry works even better after dinner. This recipe makes a sizable amount, but no one can eat just one of these bite-sized fritters, so invite some friends over and dig in.

MAKES ABOUT 40 BEIGNETS

½ cup (4 fl oz/125 ml) heavy cream

¼ cup (2 oz/60 g) granulated sugar

2 Tbsp unsalted butter, at room temperature, plus more for greasing

1 large egg, beaten

1 package (2½ tsp) rapid-rise instant yeast

3 cups (19 oz/590 g) all-purpose flour, plus more as needed and for dusting

½ tsp salt

Canola oil for deep-frying

Confectioners' sugar

Dark Chocolate Sauce (page 250) for dipping

In the bowl of a stand mixer fitted with the paddle attachment, combine ¾ cup (6 fl oz/180 ml) cold water, the cream, sugar, butter, egg, and yeast. Add 3 cups (15 oz/470 g) of the flour and the salt. With the mixer on medium-low speed, add more flour to make a soft dough that does not stick to the bowl. Remove the paddle attachment and fit the mixer with the dough hook. Knead the dough on medium-low speed, adding more flour if needed, until it is smooth but still soft, 6–7 minutes. Shape into a ball.

Lightly butter a large bowl. Add the dough and turn to coat with the butter. Cover the bowl tightly with plastic wrap. Let the dough rise in a warm spot until doubled, 1½–2 hours. Or, refrigerate overnight until doubled, 8–12 hours; remove from the refrigerator 1 hour before proceeding.

Line 2 baking sheets with parchment paper. Punch down the dough, turn it out onto a floured work surface, and dust the top with flour. Roll out into a large rectangle about ¼ inch (6 mm) thick. Using a pizza wheel or a sharp knife, cut it diagonally into 2-inch (5-cm) strips, and then again in the other direction, to create diamond shapes. Place on the baking sheets and cover loosely with plastic wrap. Let stand in a warm spot until puffy, about 15 minutes.

Preheat the oven to 200°F (95°C). Place a wire rack over a rimmed baking sheet. In a deep, heavy saucepan, pour the oil to a depth of at least 3 inches (7.5 cm) and heat to 350°F (180°C) on a deep-frying thermometer.

Using a metal spatula, lower a few of the beignets into the hot oil without crowding the pan. Turn the beignets often until puffed and golden brown, about 3 minutes. Using the skimmer, transfer them to the prepared rack to drain. Keep warm in the oven. Repeat until all of the beignets have been fried. Dust with confectioners' sugar and serve alongside a bowl of the chocolate sauce for dipping.

Soft Chocolate Mini Cakes

These molten mouthfuls are always a favorite. While not super sweet, this version has a deep chocolate flavor and is rich enough to share. The success of these cakes depends on two things: the best-quality chocolate and not overcooking them. You want the centers to be almost runny. Serve them in the ramekins or unmolded and oozing slightly.

SERVES 6

5 Tbsp (2½ oz/75 g) unsalted butter, cut into small cubes, plus more for greasing

8 oz (250 g) bittersweet chocolate, chopped

½ cup (4 oz/125 g) sugar

2 large eggs

1½ tsp vanilla extract

Salt

¼ cup (1½ oz/45 g) all-purpose flour

Whipped cream, crème fraîche, or vanilla ice cream for serving (optional)

Position a rack on the lowest level in the oven and preheat to 400°F (200°C). Lightly butter six ½-cup (4–fl oz/125-g) ramekins if serving in the ramekins. If unmolding to serve on plates, line the bottom of each ramekin with a parchment paper round.

Combine the butter and chocolate in a heatproof bowl and place over (not touching) simmering water in a saucepan. Heat until melted, then stir until smooth. Remove from the heat and let cool slightly.

Meanwhile, in a bowl, combine the sugar, eggs, vanilla, and salt. Using an electric mixer on high speed, beat until thickened, about 3 minutes. Reduce the speed to low. Gradually sprinkle the flour over the batter and continue beating just until combined. Using a spatula, fold the egg mixture into the cooled chocolate mixture until combined.

Divide the batter among the ramekins. Place the ramekins on a rimmed baking sheet and bake until the tops are puffed and dry and a toothpick inserted into the center comes out with some soft batter clinging to it, about 10 minutes.

If unmolding onto individual plates, immediately grasp a ramekin with a pot holder or thick towel, run a thin-bladed knife around the inside edge to loosen the cake, invert onto the plate, peel off the parchment, and repeat with the remaining cakes. Serve the cakes hot, topped with a dollop of whipped cream, if you like.

kitchen classics

Sturdy porcelain ramekins have many uses: they travel easily from oven to table, come in handy for serving salty nibbles, and can even work as table décor, with a single bright blossom floating in each one.

simple elegance

Pavlova is among the best dinner-party desserts because it looks so spectacular but is deceptively easy to make.

Pavlova with Summer Berries

This meringue dessert, named after Russian ballerina Anna Pavlova, has a crisp crust and soft, sometimes chewy interior. It makes an easy backdrop for a mix of seasonal fruit and softly whipped cream. When in season, fresh currants and elderflower or other edible blossoms make an especially lovely garnish.

SERVES 6–8

4 large egg whites

1 Tbsp cornstarch

1 cup (8 oz/250 g) sugar

1 tsp fresh lemon juice

1 tsp vanilla extract

1 cup (8 fl oz/250 ml) heavy cream

3 cups (12 oz/375 g) assorted fresh fruit (such as blackberries, sliced strawberries, pitted and halved cherries, and fresh currants)

Position a rack in the lower third of the oven and preheat to 300°F (150°C). Draw a 9-inch (23-cm) circle on a sheet of parchment paper. Turn the parchment paper over and place on a baking sheet.

In a bowl, using an electric mixer on medium speed, beat the egg whites until well mixed. Sprinkle the cornstarch over the whites and continue to beat until the whites are white and foamy. Raise the speed to high and very gradually add the sugar, beating until stiff, shiny peaks form. Quickly beat in the lemon juice and vanilla. Spread the meringue inside the circle drawn on the parchment, building up the edges slightly to form a rim.

Bake until the meringue is crispy, about 40 minutes. Turn off the oven and open the door. When the meringue is completely cool, remove it from the oven. Remove the parchment paper from the meringue. Place the meringue on a serving plate.

Using the electric mixer, whip the cream until soft peaks form. Spoon about three-quarters of the cream into the hollow of the meringue. Top with the berries. Cut into wedges and serve, passing the remaining whipped cream at the table.

CHAPTER FOUR

HOLIDAY CELEBRATIONS

Great memories are created around the table

When a special occasion
calls for an upscale touch,
try the classic combination
of fresh oysters on the
half shell and a vintage
Champagne or perfectly
chilled martinis—shaken
or stirred.

Oysters Mignonette

Chilled mignonette sauce, a classic accompaniment to oysters on the half shell, heightens the flavor of raw shellfish. Serve a variety of oysters, such as small, sweet Kumamotos, Malpeques, and a local type.

SERVES 6–8

FOR THE MIGNONETTE SAUCE

⅔ cup (5 fl oz/160 ml) Champagne vinegar

2 Tbsp fresh lemon juice

2 Tbsp minced shallot

Coarse salt and coarsely ground pepper

24 oysters

Crushed ice

To make the sauce, in a small serving bowl, stir together the vinegar, lemon juice, and shallot. Season to taste with salt and pepper. Cover and refrigerate until serving.

Scrub and rinse the oysters well under cold running water. Cover a large serving tray with crushed ice. Working with 1 oyster at a time, use a thick folded cloth to hold the oyster in one hand, with the flat top shell facing up. Using an oyster knife in the other hand, insert the tip between the shells near the hinge of the oyster. Twist the knife with a bit of strength to break the hinge. Run the knife along the inside surface of the top shell to loosen the oyster from it. Lift off and discard the top shell. Run the knife along the inside surface of the bottom shell to sever the muscle that attaches the oyster to the shell, then nest the oyster in its bottom shell in the ice. Repeat with the remaining oysters.

Place the bowl of sauce on the serving tray with the oysters and serve.

Almonds Spiced with Chile & Lime

Toasted and spiced nuts make a perfect party nibble. This rendition yields nuts that are both spicy and tangy, thanks to the lime juice. You can also experiment with other flavor combinations, such as sesame oil and honey or soy sauce and wasabi.

SERVES 6–8

1½ cups (8 oz/250 g) whole raw almonds

3 Tbsp fresh lime juice

1 tsp olive oil or canola oil

1 tsp chili powder

½ tsp salt

½ tsp firmly packed light brown sugar

¼ tsp cayenne pepper

Preheat the oven to 300°F (150°C). Spread the almonds in a single layer on a baking sheet and toast until lightly browned and fragrant, about 15 minutes.

Meanwhile, in a bowl, stir together the lime juice, oil, chili powder, salt, brown sugar, and cayenne. Add the almonds to the bowl hot out of the oven and stir to coat thoroughly. Leave the oven on and reserve the baking sheet.

Let the nuts cool for about 5 minutes, stirring every minute or so. Using a slotted spoon, transfer the almonds to the reserved baking sheet, discarding any remaining liquid. Bake until golden brown and dry, 8–10 minutes longer. Let cool completely on the pan. Serve immediately, or store in an airtight container at room temperature for up to 1 week.

Warm Dates with Parmesan & Walnuts

The dense texture and sweet taste of dates pair nicely with salty Parmesan and earthy, crunchy walnuts. Seek out Medjool dates for their large size, rich flavor, and tender flesh. You can assemble this easy appetizer up to 8 hours in advance and heat just before serving.

SERVES 6–8

24 large dates, preferably Medjool

2 tsp extra-virgin olive oil or walnut oil, plus more for drizzling

2 oz (60 g) Parmesan cheese, preferably Parmigiano-Reggiano

24 walnut halves

Preheat the oven to 350°F (180°C).

Using a paring knife, make a small lengthwise incision in each date and carefully remove the pit. In a bowl, gently toss the pitted dates with the olive oil. Arrange the dates, slit side up, in a single layer on a rimmed baking sheet or shallow baking dish. Using a vegetable peeler, cut the cheese into bite-size shavings. Tuck a cheese shaving or two and a walnut half into each date.

Bake until warmed through, about 10 minutes. Transfer to a serving platter, drizzle with more oil, and serve.

Potato-Apple Pancakes with Smoked Trout

These savory pancakes are ideal for entertaining, as they can be held in a warm oven for up to a half hour before serving. Make the assembly a team effort: while one person grates the apples and potatoes, the other one can ready the remaining ingredients and the equipment.

MAKES 24 (3-INCH/7.5-CM) PANCAKES; SERVES 12

4 russet potatoes, about 2 lb (1 kg) total weight, peeled

2 Granny Smith, pippin, or Gravenstein apples, peeled, cored, and grated, plus 2 whole apples for garnish

1 large egg, lightly beaten

½ cup (2½ oz/75 g) all-purpose flour

Salt and freshly ground pepper

2 Tbsp unsalted butter, plus more as needed

2 Tbsp olive oil, plus more as needed

1½ cups (12 oz/375 g) crème fraîche or sour cream

¾ lb (375 g) smoked trout

½ cup (4 oz/125 g) salmon roe

Fresh chervil leaves for garnish

Preheat the oven to 200°F (95°C). Using the large holes on a box grater, shred the potatoes into a colander. Press out any excess liquid, then transfer the potatoes to a large bowl. Stir in the grated apples, egg, and flour until well mixed. Season with 1 teaspoon salt and ½ teaspoon pepper.

On a griddle or in a large nonstick frying pan over medium heat, melt the butter with the olive oil. Working in batches, add 3 tablespoon-size mounds of the potato mixture to the pan without crowding and, using a spatula, press down firmly on each mound to form 3-inch pancakes. Cook, turning once, until golden brown on both sides, 8–10 minutes total. Place the pancakes in a single layer on a baking sheet and keep warm in the oven. Add more butter and oil to the pan as needed and repeat until all of the potato mixture is used.

Core and quarter the remaining 2 apples and cut each quarter into 6 thin wedges.

Garnish each warm pancake with 1 tablespoon crème fraîche, a piece of smoked trout, 1 teaspoon salmon roe, 2 apple slices, and a few chervil leaves, and serve.

holiday classics

Potato latkes, a Hanukkah staple, should always be served warm and crispy on the outside. Going all out with savory toppings, as in this recipe, transforms them from something everyday into the anchor for an indulgent wintertime feast.

HOLIDAYS YOUR WAY

COZY, FESTIVE GATHERINGS *are hallmarks of the winter season, with opportunities to* **CELEBRATE FRIENDSHIPS** *new and old and to bring family and friends together.*

CREATING YOUR OWN TRADITIONS *is part of the fun. You can easily borrow a few classics from your childhood, like that favorite cranberry relish, while also letting your personal style inform the* **MENU AND DECOR.** *A simple table dressed in silver and white is an unfussy way to host a special event and capture the* **SPIRIT OF THE HOLIDAYS.**

Seared Scallops with Bacon Vinaigrette

Frisée, a curly-edged, hearty chicory variety, stands up well to a warm dressing like this smoky bacon vinaigrette laced with Dijon mustard and sherry vinegar. Top the greens with rich, buttery scallops, and you'll have a salad worthy of any special occasion.

SERVES 8

8 slices bacon

1 cup (5 oz/155 g) finely chopped shallots

4 cloves garlic, minced

2 Tbsp Dijon mustard

6 Tbsp (3 fl oz/90 ml) sherry vinegar

⅔ cup (5 fl oz/160 ml) plus 2 Tbsp extra-virgin olive oil, plus more as needed

2 Tbsp sugar

Salt and freshly ground pepper

24 large sea scallops, about 1½ lb (750 g) total weight

1 lb (500 g) frisée, torn into bite-size pieces

In a large sauté pan over medium-high heat, fry the bacon until crisp, about 5 minutes. Transfer to paper towels to drain. When the bacon is cool enough to handle, crumble it into a large bowl and set aside. Drain off all but 3 tablespoons of the bacon fat from the pan. (If you have less than 3 tablespoons, supplement with olive oil.)

Return the pan to medium heat. Add the shallots and sauté until lightly browned, 2–3 minutes. Add the garlic and cook for another minute. Remove from the heat and whisk in the mustard, vinegar, ⅔ cup (5 fl oz/160 ml) of the olive oil, and the sugar to make a vinaigrette. Season to taste with salt and pepper and set aside.

Remove the tough muscle from the side of each scallop if necessary. Pat the scallops dry and season with salt and pepper. In a frying pan over medium-high heat, warm 1½ teaspoons of the olive oil. Arrange 6 of the scallops in the pan without crowding and sauté, turning once, until golden and just cooked through, 1–2 minutes per side. Transfer the scallops to a plate. Repeat 3 more times, adding another 1½ teaspoons olive oil and another 6 scallops each time.

Add the frisée to the bowl with the bacon. Reheat the vinaigrette over low heat until warm, about 1 minute. Pour three-fourths of the vinaigrette over the greens and toss to coat. Divide the salad evenly among individual plates. Top with the scallops, drizzle with the remaining vinaigrette, and serve.

Blood Orange, Avocado & Crab Salad

Crabmeat from a freshly cooked crab is available during crab season at many seafood counters. Dungeness crabmeat is recommended here, but you can substitute any good-quality lump crabmeat, such as king or spider crab.

SERVES 6

4 blood oranges

2 tsp white wine vinegar

1 Tbsp minced shallot

1 Tbsp minced fresh chives

Salt and freshly ground pepper

3 Tbsp extra-virgin olive oil

4 cups (6 oz/180 g) mixed torn frisée and radicchio leaves

½ lb (250 g) fresh lump crabmeat

2 firm but ripe avocados, cut into ½-inch (12-mm) slices

Using a small, sharp knife, cut a slice off both ends of the blood oranges to reveal the flesh. Stand a blood orange upright on a cutting board and cut off the peel and pith in strips, cutting downward and following the contour of the fruit. Holding the blood orange in one hand over a bowl, cut along either side of each section to release it from the membrane, letting the sections drop into the bowl. Pour any juice that collects in the bowl into the vinaigrette. Repeat with the remaining blood oranges.

In a small bowl, whisk together 2 teaspoons of the blood orange juice with the vinegar, shallot, chives, and a pinch each of salt and pepper. Whisking constantly, slowly add the oil until well combined to make a vinaigrette.

In a bowl, toss the lettuce with 1 tablespoon of the vinaigrette. Divide the lettuce leaves among 6 salad plates. Place the oranges and crabmeat in the bowl and drizzle with all but 1 tablespoon of the remaining vinaigrette. Toss to coat evenly, then arrange the orange-crabmeat mixture over the lettuce on each plate, dividing it evenly. Toss the avocado with the remaining 1 tablespoon vinaigrette, then arrange on top of each salad. Season with salt and pepper and serve.

A mandoline is the ideal tool for shaving paper-thin slices of fuyu persimmon or other fruits. If you don't have one, try a serrated peeler for soft-skinned vegetables instead.

Shaved Persimmon Salad with Endive & Pomegranate

Serve this crisp and refreshing salad in the fall, when persimmons and pomegranates are in season. Fuyu persimmons are sweet, firm, and easy to cut very thin. Any salty or tangy cheese will do—try using fresh ricotta salata or goat cheese in place of the feta.

SERVES 4

4 heads Belgian endive,
a mix of red and white

1 large pomegranate

2 Fuyu persimmons

8 oz (250 g) feta cheese, crumbled

Grated zest and juice of 1 lemon

1 tsp Champagne vinegar

Salt and freshly ground pepper

½ cup (4 fl oz/125 ml) extra-virgin olive oil

Trim the ends from the endives, separate the leaves, and place in a large bowl. Seed the pomegranate and pat the seeds dry. Using a mandoline or a very sharp knife, thinly slice the persimmons. Add the pomegranate seeds, persimmons, and cheese to the endive leaves.

In a small bowl, whisk together the lemon zest, lemon juice, and vinegar. Season to taste with salt and pepper. Add the olive oil in a thin stream, whisking constantly, until the dressing is smooth. Drizzle the vinaigrette over the salad and gently toss. Season to taste with salt and pepper and serve.

Crottin Salad
with Pears,
Fennel & Currants

Try different cheeses in place of the crottin: any aged goat's milk cheese will be delicious. Serve with a crisp, minerally white wine, such as Sancerre, Pouilly-Fumé, or Sauvignon Blanc.

SERVES 4–6

2 fennel bulbs, trimmed and any fronds reserved

1 Tbsp sherry vinegar

1 aged Crottin de Chavignol or other small, round aged goat cheese, about 2 oz (60 g), grated

Salt and ground white pepper

3 Tbsp extra-virgin olive oil

1½ cups (1½ oz/45 g) mâche, field greens, or baby arugula

3 pears, halved, cored, and thinly sliced

⅓ cup (2 oz/60 g) dried currants

Using a mandoline or a very sharp knife, cut each fennel bulb lengthwise into paper-thin slices. Then, using a knife, cut each slice lengthwise into strips ¼ inch (6 mm) wide.

In a large bowl, using a fork, mix together the vinegar, 1 tablespoon of the cheese, ½ teaspoon salt, and ¼ teaspoon white pepper. Add the oil in a thin stream, whisking constantly, until the dressing is well combined. Add the fennel and toss to coat.

Divide the mâche among the plates. Top each plate of mâche equally with fennel, pears, and currants. Sprinkle with the remaining cheese, garnish with a few fennel fronds, and serve.

Roasted Parsnip & Apple Soup with Gruyère Toasts

Parsnips and apples are a great flavor pairing: the apples brighten the earthiness of the parsnips. Don't skip the melted Gruyère toasts in this recipe. Dipping them into the soup is a delicious experience.

SERVES 4–6

6 parsnips, peeled and chopped
(about 4 cups/1¼ lb/625 g)

1 Tbsp olive oil

Salt and freshly ground black pepper

3 Tbsp unsalted butter

1 small yellow onion, chopped

¼ tsp freshly grated nutmeg

2 Granny Smith apples, peeled, cored,
and chopped, plus apple slices for garnish

6 cups (48 fl oz/1.5 l) chicken broth

Ground white pepper

FOR THE GRUYÈRE TOASTS

4 oz (125 g) Gruyère cheese,
shredded

1 loaf crusty bread, cut into
slices ¼ inch (6 mm) thick

Preheat the oven to 400°F (200°C). Line a baking sheet with parchment paper. In a bowl, toss the parsnips with the oil and season with salt and black pepper. Arrange in a single layer on the prepared pan and roast until beginning to caramelize, 25 minutes.

In a large, heavy pot over medium-high heat, melt the butter. Add the onion and sauté until translucent, about 5 minutes. Add the nutmeg and cook for 1 minute. Add the chopped apples, stir to coat, and cook until beginning to soften, about 5 minutes. Add the broth and parsnips and bring to a boil. Reduce the heat to low and simmer, uncovered, until the parsnips are tender, about 20 minutes. Remove from the heat and let cool slightly.

Working in batches, purée the soup in a blender. Return to the pot and season with salt and white pepper.

To make the toasts, preheat the broiler to high. Put 2 tablespoons of the cheese on each bread slice. Arrange the slices on the baking sheet and broil until the cheese begins to melt, 2–3 minutes.

Serve the soup, garnished with apple slices. Place 1 or 2 Gruyère toasts on the side of each bowl.

autumn hues

This soup brings the warm colors of fall to the table. Look to seasonal ingredients like squash and gourds for decor inspiration as well, incorporating them into place settings or a festive centerpiece.

Squash Soup with Thyme Cream

Roasting the squash gives this comforting golden soup a lush, velvety texture, and the thyme adds an earthy flavor note. Place wide, shallow soup bowls atop chargers or dinner plates so the table will not look empty between the soup course and the main course.

SERVES 8–10

½ cup (4 oz/125 g) crème fraîche or sour cream

1 tsp minced fresh thyme, plus sprigs for garnish

Ground white pepper

2 large winter squash such as butternut, 3–4 lb (1.75–2 kg) total weight, halved and seeded

6 Tbsp (3 oz/90 g) unsalted butter

Salt and freshly ground black pepper

1 yellow onion, chopped

5 cups (40 fl oz/1.25 l) chicken broth

1 cup (8 fl oz/250 ml) heavy cream

easy garnishes

Creamy squash soup is an ideal canvas for a variety of garnishes. In lieu of the thyme cream, try a spoonful of any of the following:

• Parmesan breadcrumbs (page 196)

• Herb-almond pesto (page 193)

• Romesco sauce (page 69)

• Crispy shallots and chiles (page 196)

• Smoky tomato salsa (page 73)

• Harissa (page 93)

• Bacon, onions, and parsley (page 197)

Preheat the oven to 350°F (180°C). Line a large rimmed baking sheet with aluminum foil.

In a small bowl, whisk together the crème fraîche, thyme, and ⅛ teaspoon white pepper. Cover and refrigerate until serving.

Place the squash halves, cut side up, on the prepared baking sheet. Put 1 tablespoon of the butter in each squash cavity and season the squash with salt and black pepper. Roast until tender, about 45 minutes. (At this point, the squash can be refrigerated for up to 1 day. Bring to room temperature before proceeding.)

In a large saucepan over low heat, melt the remaining 2 tablespoons butter. Add the onion and cook, stirring occasionally, until softened but not browned, about 5 minutes. Scoop the squash flesh out of the skins into the saucepan, then add the broth and stir until smooth. Bring to a simmer over medium heat. Cook, stirring occasionally, until reduced by about one-fourth, about 30 minutes. Remove from the heat and let cool, uncovered, until just warm.

Working in batches if necessary, purée the soup in a blender or food processor or with a stick blender until completely smooth. (At this point, the soup can stand for up to 1 hour at room temperature or be covered and refrigerated for up to 6 hours.)

Strain the soup through a fine-mesh sieve into a clean saucepan and stir in the cream, 1 teaspoon salt, and a pinch of white pepper. Rewarm the soup over low heat. Taste and adjust the seasoning.

Ladle into bowls, gently swirl about 1 teaspoon of the thyme cream into the center of each bowl, garnish with thyme sprigs, and serve.

Cider-Brined Spice-Rubbed Turkey

Treating your turkey to an apple cider brine sweetened with maple syrup produces wonderfully juicy, flavorful meat, and the spice rub delivers yet another layer of flavor. The turkey is slipped into the brine 36 to 48 hours before it goes in the oven, so be sure to plan ahead.

SERVES 8–12

FOR THE BRINE

8 cups (64 fl oz/2 l) apple cider

¾ cup (6 oz/185 g) kosher salt

1 cup (8 fl oz/250 ml) maple syrup or sorghum syrup

2 bay leaves

2 sprigs fresh rosemary

3 sprigs fresh thyme

6 juniper berries

5 allspice berries

1 turkey, 12–14 lb (6–7 kg), neck and giblets removed

FOR THE SPICE RUB

¼ cup (2 oz/60 g) sumac

2 Tbsp kosher salt

2 Tbsp turmeric

2 tsp ground cinnamon

½ tsp freshly ground pepper

¼ tsp ground cloves

¼ cup (2 fl oz/60 ml) olive oil or canola oil

To make the brine, in a large saucepan over high heat, combine 8 cups (64 fl oz/2 l) water, the cider, salt, and maple syrup. Bring to a boil, stirring to dissolve the salt. Remove from the heat. Add the bay leaves, rosemary, thyme, juniper berries, and allspice to the pan. Let cool.

Place the turkey in a nonreactive pot or brining bag large enough to hold the whole turkey. Carefully add the brine plus enough water to submerge the turkey completely in liquid. Cover and refrigerate for 24–36 hours.

Remove the turkey from the brine, rinse with cold water, and pat dry with paper towels (discard the brine). Place the turkey on a large rimmed baking sheet. Refrigerate, uncovered, for 12 hours.

About 1 hour before cooking, remove the turkey from the refrigerator and let stand at room temperature.

Position a rack in the lower third of the oven and preheat to 450°F (230°C).

To make the spice rub, in a bowl, combine the sumac, salt, turmeric, cinnamon, pepper, and cloves.

Brush the turkey all over with the oil and use your hands to rub the spice rub evenly over the surface of the bird. Place the turkey, breast side up, on a rack in a large roasting pan. Place in the oven and reduce the oven temperature to 400°F (200°C). Roast for 30 minutes.

Reduce the temperature to 350°F (180°C). Continue to roast until the skin is golden brown, 2–2½ hours longer. Insert an instant-read thermometer into the thickest part of the breast and thigh away from the bone. The breast should register 165°F (74°C) and the thigh 175°F (80°C).

Place the turkey on a carving board, cover loosely with aluminum foil, and let rest for 20–30 minutes before carving.

lovely garnish
When it comes to fresh decor for your serving platter, look no farther than your own backyard or local market. Edible blooms, such as the lavender and fennel used here, are beautiful adornments.

Maple-Mustard Turkey with Cranberry Relish

Sweet and slightly smoky maple syrup is an easy way to add full, complex flavor to both sweet and savory dishes. Here, it balances the spiciness of mustard to make a simple glaze for lean turkey tenderloins. A splash of full-bodied port contributes to a bold sauce.

SERVES 4–6

2 turkey tenderloins, about ¾ lb (375 g) each

Kosher salt and freshly ground pepper

1 Tbsp unsalted butter

2 Tbsp maple syrup

1 Tbsp Dijon mustard

1¾ cups (7 oz/220 g) fresh cranberries

½ cup (4 fl oz/125 ml) tawny or ruby port

½ cup (4 oz/125 g) sugar

3 Tbsp minced crystallized ginger

Preheat the oven to 350°F (180°C). Using kitchen string, tie each tenderloin crosswise in 3 or 4 places, spacing the ties evenly. Season with 1 teaspoon salt and ½ teaspoon pepper.

In a large ovenproof frying pan over medium-high heat, melt the butter. Add the tenderloins and cook, turning occasionally, until browned on all sides, about 5 minutes total. Remove from the heat.

In a small bowl, stir together the maple syrup and mustard. Spread about half of the mixture over the tenderloins. Place the pan in the oven and cook for 10 minutes. Spread the remaining mixture over the tenderloins, return to the oven, and continue to cook until an instant-read thermometer inserted in the center of a tenderloin registers 165°F (74°C), about 10 minutes longer.

Meanwhile, in a heavy nonreactive saucepan, combine the cranberries, port, sugar, and crystallized ginger and bring to a boil over high heat, stirring often. Reduce heat to medium and cook, uncovered, at a brisk simmer, stirring often, until the berries have popped and the juices are syrupy, about 10 minutes. Prepare a large bowl of ice water. When the sauce is ready, transfer it to a heatproof bowl and nest it in the ice water. Let cool, then transfer to a serving bowl.

When the tenderloins are ready, transfer them to a carving board and let rest for 5 minutes. Snip the strings and cut the tenderloins crosswise into slices ½ inch (12 mm) thick.

Divide the turkey evenly among warmed dinner plates. Spoon some cranberry sauce alongside the turkey and serve. Pass the remaining sauce at the table.

Herb-Brined Pork Loin with Apple-Ginger Compote

Cuts of pork of every kind are versatile, flavorful, simple to cook, and popular with a wide range of meat eaters—but pork is easy to overcook. This loin, made tender and juicy with an overnight brine bath and served with a sweet and savory compote, will never let the cook down.

SERVES 4–6

FOR THE BRINE

½ cup (4 oz/125 g) kosher salt

½ cup (3½ oz/105 g) firmly packed light brown sugar

1 Tbsp freshly ground pepper

1 yellow onion, finely chopped

5 cloves garlic, crushed

3 sprigs fresh thyme, plus 2 tsp chopped thyme

3 sprigs fresh rosemary, plus 2 tsp chopped rosemary

1 boneless center-cut pork loin, about 3 lb (1.5 kg), rolled and tied by the butcher

Olive oil for rubbing

FOR THE COMPOTE

2 Tbsp unsalted butter

1 large yellow onion, thinly sliced

¼ tsp kosher salt

2 Granny Smith or other tart green apples, peeled, cored, and diced

⅓ cup (2 oz/60 g) golden raisins

2 Tbsp apricot jam

1 tsp peeled and grated fresh ginger

½ tsp dry mustard

4 drops Tabasco or other hot-pepper sauce

Pinch of ground white pepper

½ cup (4 fl oz/125 ml) dry white wine

To make the brine, in a large saucepan, combine the salt, brown sugar, pepper, onion, garlic, and herb sprigs. Pour in 3 cups (24 fl oz/750 ml) water and place over medium heat. Stir until the salt and sugar dissolve. Pour 6 cups (48 fl oz/ 1.5 l) cold water into a large metal or glass container. Add the salt-sugar mixture and stir to combine. Let cool.

Carefully submerge the pork loin in the brine, adding cold water if needed to cover the pork. Cover and refrigerate for at least 3 hours or up to 24 hours.

Preheat the oven to 350°F (180°C). Remove the pork from the brine and pat dry with paper towels (discard the brine). Rub all over with olive oil. Sprinkle with the chopped herbs, pressing them into the meat so they adhere.

Place the pork, fat side up, in a roasting pan and roast for 30 minutes. Turn over the pork and continue roasting until an instant-read thermometer inserted into the thickest part registers 140°F (60°C), about 20 minutes longer.

Meanwhile, make the compote: In a frying pan over medium heat, melt the butter. Add the onion and salt and sauté until lightly golden, 8–10 minutes. Add the apples, raisins, jam, ginger, mustard, hot-pepper sauce, and white pepper to the pan and stir to combine. Pour in the wine, bring to a boil, then reduce the heat to low. Cover and simmer, stirring occasionally, until the apples are soft, about 10 minutes. Transfer to a serving bowl and set aside.

Turn the pork again and raise the oven temperature to 450°F (230°C). Roast until the top is browned, about 5 minutes longer. Transfer the pork to a cutting board, tent with aluminum foil, and let rest for 10–15 minutes. Cut into slices and serve with the compote.

MERRY AND BRIGHT

There's no need to use Grandmother's china if you're a couple

who likes to focus on what's **MODERN AND DIFFERENT.**

Try farmhouse style, with rustic napkins and no-frills

food presentation brightened by **SEASONAL TOUCHES** *like*

winter citrus. What sets the holidays apart is the chance

to **BUILD NEW TRADITIONS** *the two of you will always*

cherish. Be bold and experiment with what you like until

each special occasion **FEELS DISTINCTLY YOUR OWN.**

Beef Tenderloin with Wild Mushrooms

If your market does not have fresh chanterelle, maitake, morel, or other wild mushrooms, substitute flavorful domesticated varieties, such as oyster, shiitake, or cremini.

SERVES 8

1 oz (30 g) dried porcini mushrooms

1½ cups (12 fl oz/375 ml) very hot water

1½ lb (750 g) wild mushrooms, stems removed

2 Tbsp unsalted butter plus 3 Tbsp melted unsalted butter

3 large shallots, minced

Salt and freshly ground pepper

½ cup (4 fl oz/125 ml) brandy or Cognac

1 can (15 fl oz/470 ml) beef consommé

1 beef tenderloin, about 3½ lb (1.75 kg)

1–2 tsp coarsely cracked peppercorns

1 cup (8 fl oz/250 ml) heavy cream

1 tsp white or black truffle oil

Soak the porcini in the hot water for 20 minutes. Meanwhile, slice the mushrooms. Drain the porcini through a coffee filter into a small pitcher and reserve the soaking water. Squeeze the excess water from the porcini and chop finely.

In a large saucepan over medium heat, melt the 2 tablespoons butter. Add the shallots and sauté until softened, 4–5 minutes. Add the porcini and the wild mushrooms, season with salt and pepper, and cook, stirring occasionally, until they release moisture, about 10 minutes. Add the brandy, raise the heat to high, and bring to a simmer. Stir until the liquid has almost completely evaporated, about 5 minutes. Add the porcini soaking water and the consommé, adjust the heat so the liquid simmers briskly, and cook, uncovered, for about 30 minutes.

If the roast has a skinny end, fold it under and tie with string to create a uniform diameter. Pat the roast dry and place it on a rack on a rimmed baking sheet. Brush all over with the melted butter and season generously with salt and cracked peppercorns, pressing gently to help the seasoning adhere. Let stand at room temperature for 30–60 minutes.

Preheat the oven to 450°F (230°C). Roast the beef until an instant-read thermometer inserted into the thickest part reads 115°F (46°C) for rare, or 125°F (52°C) for medium-rare. Start checking the temperature after 20 minutes. Place the beef on a cutting board, tent with foil, and let rest for 10 minutes.

Meanwhile, finish the sauce. Whisk the cream into the sauce, season lightly with salt and pepper, and simmer over medium-low heat until slightly thickened, 10–15 minutes. Remove from the heat. Taste and adjust the seasoning. Whisk in the truffle oil, cover, and set aside until ready to serve.

Cut the beef into thick slices and place on a platter. Spoon some of the mushroom sauce over the sliced beef. Pass the remaining sauce at the table.

wine pairing

A generously-seasoned special occasion roast like this one can stand up to a deep, full-bodied red, such as Cabernet Sauvignon or other Bordeaux-type blends.

Rib Roast with Horseradish Sauce

Seasoned with mustard, rosemary, and thyme and served with a Madeira jus, this standing rib roast is a traditional Christmas dish in Britain. If you are serving this for a special-occasion meal, ask the butcher to remove the roast's chine bone to ease carving and to shorten and french the ribs for a striking presentation.

SERVES 6

2 Tbsp Dijon mustard

1 Tbsp olive oil

1 Tbsp chopped fresh thyme leaves

1 Tbsp chopped fresh rosemary leaves

2 cloves garlic, chopped

Salt and freshly ground pepper

1 standing rib roast, about 6–6½ lb (3–3.25 kg), frenched

FOR THE HORSERADISH SAUCE

½ cup (4 fl oz/125 ml) heavy cream

2 Tbsp prepared horseradish

½ tsp Dijon mustard

Salt

3 or 4 drops hot-pepper sauce

FOR THE MADEIRA JUS

2 cups (16 fl oz/500 ml) dry Madeira

2 Tbsp beef or veal demi-glace

In a small bowl, stir together the mustard, olive oil, thyme, rosemary, and garlic with 1 tablespoon salt and 2 teaspoons pepper to form a paste. Rub the paste all over the roast and let stand at room temperature for 1 hour.

Position a rack in the lower third of the oven and preheat the oven to 450°F (230°C). Place the roast, bone side down, in a roasting pan and roast for 15 minutes. Reduce the oven temperature to 350°F (180°C) and continue to roast until an instant-read thermometer inserted into the thickest part away from the bone registers 130°F (54°C) for medium-rare, about 1¾ hours longer, or until done to your liking. Transfer the roast to a warmed serving platter and tent with aluminum foil. Let rest for 15–20 minutes.

Meanwhile, make the horseradish sauce: In a small bowl, whisk the cream until soft peaks form. Fold in the horseradish, mustard, ¼ teaspoon salt, and the hot-pepper sauce. Spoon the sauce into a serving bowl and refrigerate until serving.

To make the Madeira jus, use a large spoon to skim off the fat from the drippings in the roasting pan. Place the roasting pan over medium-high heat and stir the Madeira into the pan juices, scraping up the brown bits from the pan bottom. Whisk in the demi-glace and any meat juices from the serving platter. Continue to cook, stirring occasionally, until the liquid is reduced by half, 8–10 minutes longer. Pour the jus through a fine-mesh sieve into a warmed serving bowl and skim off any fat that rises to the surface.

Carve the roast tableside. Arrange on warmed individual plates and serve, passing the horseradish sauce and the jus at the table.

Baked Ham with Spiced Cider Glaze

A whole baked ham is a welcome sight on the holiday table, and it is easy to prepare. Carve the ham at the dining table and serve each guest, or set the sliced ham on a buffet and let guests serve themselves. If you have leftover ham, use it to make ham sandwiches with your favorite mustard, or chop it into small pieces and add to a frittata.

SERVES 10–12

1 cup (8 fl oz/250 ml) apple cider

2 cinnamon sticks

20–25 whole cloves

3 star anise

1 fully cooked bone-in ham, about 8 lb (4 kg)

½ cup (3½ oz/105 g) firmly packed light brown sugar

¼ cup (3 oz/90 g) honey

2 tsp dry mustard

Fresh herb sprigs for garnish

Preheat the oven to 325°F (165°C).

In a small saucepan over medium-high heat, combine the cider, cinnamon sticks, 6 of the cloves, and the star anise. Bring to a boil, reduce the heat to low, cover, and simmer for 15 minutes. Remove from the heat. (At this point, the cider can be covered and refrigerated for up to 24 hours.)

Cut away and discard any skin on the ham and trim the fat to ½ inch (12 mm) thick. Using a sharp knife, score the fat on the upper half of the ham in a crosshatch pattern, cutting about ¼ inch (6 mm) deep. Stick the remaining cloves at the corners of the crosshatch pattern. Line a shallow roasting pan with foil, then place a rack in the pan. Place the ham, fat side up, on the rack. Bake for 1¼ hours.

In a small bowl, combine the brown sugar, honey, and mustard and mix well. Pat half of the mixture over the scored surface of the ham. Stir the spiced cider into the remaining half of the mixture. Continue to bake, basting several times with the cider mixture, until the ham is glazed and shining, about 1 hour longer.

Transfer the ham to a carving board and tent with foil. Let rest for 15 minutes. Carve the ham and arrange on a warmed platter. Garnish with herb sprigs and serve.

kitchen staple

Pesto is an indispensable recipe in any cook's repertoire because it pairs well with many dishes beyond pasta, such as these pan-seared lamb chops or appetizers like flatbread or roasted vegetables.

Pan-Seared Lamb Chops with Herb-Almond Pesto

A bright green, tangy herb sauce beautifully complements the rich flavor of these seared lamb chops. Seek out sustainably raised lamb, preferably from a local farm, for the best quality. Pour a good Cabernet Sauvignon or red Bordeaux at the table.

SERVES 4

FOR THE HERB-ALMOND PESTO

1½ cups (1½ oz/45 g) lightly packed fresh basil leaves

1 cup (1 oz/30 g) lightly packed fresh flat-leaf parsley leaves

½ cup (½ oz/15 g) lightly packed fresh mint leaves

3 Tbsp slivered almonds, lightly toasted

2 cloves garlic, chopped

Salt

¾ cup (6 fl oz/180 ml) extra-virgin olive oil

2 tsp balsamic vinegar

FOR THE LAMB CHOPS

8 double-cut lamb chops

Salt and freshly ground pepper

1 Tbsp olive oil

To make the pesto, in a food processor, combine the basil, parsley, mint, almonds, garlic, and 1 teaspoon salt. Process until coarsely chopped, stopping to scrape down the sides of the bowl as needed. With the motor running, drizzle in the olive oil and process to a thick consistency. Scrape the pesto into a bowl and stir in the vinegar. Set aside.

To prepare the lamb chops, preheat the oven to 225°F (110°C). Pat the chops dry with paper towels. Season on all sides with salt and pepper. Let stand at room temperature for 30 minutes.

Place a large, heavy frying pan over medium-high heat, add the olive oil, and heat until very hot, about 2 minutes. Add the chops and sear, without moving, until golden brown, 2–2½ minutes. Turn and sear for 2–2½ minutes longer. Using tongs, lift each chop and sear all the fatty edges, about 1 minute total. Transfer the pan to the oven and continue to cook until an instant-read thermometer inserted into a chop, away from the bone, registers 135°F (57°C) for medium-rare, 20–30 minutes. Transfer to a platter, tent with aluminum foil, and let rest for 5 minutes.

Arrange 2 chops on each of 4 dinner plates, spoon a generous dollop of pesto on the side, and serve.

Roasted Lobster with Garlic-Lemon Butter

The high heat of the oven intensifies the natural sweetness of lobster, which is nicely complemented by the garlic-lemon butter. To add some heat to the butter, stir in a few jalapeño slices.

SERVES 4

FOR THE GARLIC-LEMON BUTTER

½ cup (4 oz/125 g) unsalted butter

3 cloves garlic, minced

Zest and juice of 1 lemon, plus 2 lemons, halved

Kosher salt and freshly ground pepper

1 Tbsp minced fresh herbs such as chervil, flat-leaf parsley, tarragon, or any combination

¼ cup (2 oz/60 g) kosher salt

4 live Maine lobsters, 1¼–1½ lb (625–750 g) each

Lemon wedges

Jalapeño slices (optional)

claw crackers

You don't need special shellfish crackers to manage lobster claws. Any 6-inch (15-cm) swing-handled nut cracker does the trick. Plan ahead to make sure you have a cracker on hand for each guest.

To make the garlic-lemon butter, in a small saucepan over medium heat, melt the butter. Stir in the garlic and the lemon zest and juice. Add salt and pepper to taste, and the herbs. Keep warm.

Fill a large stockpot with enough water to cover the lobsters and bring to a boil. Add the ¼ cup (2 oz/60 g) salt. Leaving any rubber bands on the claws, plunge the lobsters headfirst into the water. Cover the pot and listen carefully for the water to return to a full boil, 5–6 minutes. Once the water returns to a boil, cook the lobsters, covered, until half-cooked, about 5 minutes longer.

Using tongs, remove the lobsters from the pot and rinse under cold running water. Remove any rubber bands. To drain, plunge a knife into the head of each lobster between the eyes, and hold the lobster over the sink, first by the tail, then by the claws, and then by the tail again.

Turn each lobster on its back. Using a chef's knife, cut each in half vertically, from head to tail. Holding the tails at each end, crack them so that they will lie flat. Using a spoon, remove and discard the greenish sacs just below the heads. Remove and discard the intestinal tracts that run along the bottom of the shells from head to tail. Insert a wooden skewer on one side of the large end of each lobster tail and push it to extend all the way through the tail to keep it flat while roasting. If desired, leave the tomalley and any roe.

Arrange 1 oven rack in the upper third and 1 rack in the center of the oven and preheat to 425°F (220°C). Place 4 lobster halves, cut sides up and facing opposite directions, on each of 2 baking sheets. Spread one-eighth of the garlic-lemon butter over the cut side of each half. Place the baking sheets in the oven and roast, switching the pans halfway through, until meat is opaque, about 5 minutes. Serve with lemon halves and the remaining garlic-lemon butter on the side, adding a few jalapeño slices to the butter, if desired.

holiday seafood

Not every festive celebration
calls for a meat main course.
A seafood indulgence like
whole lobster or crab makes
a memorable impression and
puts a fresh spin on the holidays.

Easy Vegetables Four Ways

crispy shallots + chiles

6 large shallots, trimmed and papery skins removed
2 jalapeños • Peanut oil • 1 lime wedge for serving (optional)

Using a very sharp knife, cut the shallots and jalapeños crosswise into thin slices and set aside. Pour the peanut oil into a small heavy pot or sauté pan and heat over medium-high heat until a deep-fry thermometer registers 325°F (170°C). Working in small batches, sprinkle the shallots and jalapeños into the oil, separating the pieces as much as possible. Fry, stirring constantly, until light golden brown, 1–1½ minutes. Using a slotted spoon, transfer the shallot mixture to a paper towel–lined plate to cool (the shallots will darken as they cool). Serve over cooked vegetables with a squeeze of lime, if you wish.

MAKES ABOUT ½ CUP (2 OZ/60 G)

parmesan + bread crumbs

1 cup (2 oz/60 g) fresh bread crumbs • 1 cup (4 oz/125 g) freshly grated Parmesan cheese • 1 Tbsp olive oil

Preheat the oven to 375°F (190°C). In a bowl, stir together the bread crumbs, cheese, and olive oil until well blended. Spread the bread-crumb mixture on a greased rimmed baking sheet. Bake until golden brown, about 15 minutes. Serve over cooked vegetables.

MAKES ABOUT 2 CUPS (8 OZ/250 G)

Fresh seasonal vegetables are great on their own but even better with a little something extra on top. These four easy, last-minute additions elevate simply prepared veggie side dishes to special-occasion fare.

fried bacon + onions + parsley

4 slices bacon • 1 Tbsp olive oil • ½ yellow onion, finely chopped
¼ cup (¼ oz/7 g) finely chopped fresh flat-leaf parsley

In a frying pan over medium heat, fry the bacon until crisp, about 5 minutes. Using tongs, transfer to a paper towel–lined plate and set aside. Pour off all but 1 tablespoon of the bacon fat from the frying pan. Add the olive oil and the onion to the pan and sauté over medium-low heat until tender, about 7 minutes. Remove from the heat, crumble in the bacon, and mix well. Just before serving, stir in the parsley, then spoon over cooked vegetables.

MAKES ABOUT ½ CUP (2 OZ/60 G)

yogurt + onions + bell pepper

1 cup (8 oz/250 g) plain Greek yogurt • 2 Tbsp finely chopped red onion • ¼ tsp grated lemon zest • 1 Tbsp fresh lemon juice
¼ cup (1½ oz/45 g) finely chopped green bell pepper
1 Tbsp olive oil • Freshly ground mixed peppercorns

In a small serving bowl, stir together the yogurt, red onion, and the lemon zest and juice; set aside. Spoon over cooked vegetables, then scatter bell pepper over the top. Drizzle with the olive oil and season well with pepper.

MAKES ABOUT 1½ CUPS (10 OZ/325 G)

Roasted Squash with Dates & Spicy Pecans

This rich salad, composed of meaty, bright yellow winter squash, honey-and-spice pecans, sweet dates, and peppery curly endive, makes a great side dish to roasted meats, pastas, or hearty soups.

SERVES 6–8

6 Tbsp (3 fl oz/90 ml) extra-virgin olive oil, plus more for greasing

1 Tbsp sugar

Salt and freshly ground black pepper

4 Tbsp (3 oz/90 g) honey

⅛ tsp cayenne pepper

¾ cup (3 oz/90 g) pecan halves

1 large acorn squash, 1½–2 lb (750 g–1 kg)

¼ cup (2 fl oz/60 ml) Champagne vinegar

1 Tbsp Dijon mustard

1 large head or 2 small heads curly endive, about 10 oz (315 g) total weight, cored, tough stems removed, and leaves torn into bite-sized pieces

¾ cup (4 oz/125 g) dates, pitted and quartered lengthwise

Preheat the oven to 325°F (165°C). Line a rimmed baking sheet with parchment paper. Lightly grease the parchment with olive oil.

In a bowl, stir together the sugar and ¼ teaspoon salt. Set aside.

In a frying pan over low heat, warm 2 tablespoons of the honey. Add the cayenne and stir to mix well. Add the pecans and stir to coat. Spread the nuts in a single layer on the prepared baking sheet and toast in the oven until fragrant and lightly browned, about 10 minutes. Remove from the oven and let cool slightly, then add the nuts to the bowl with the sugar mixture and toss to coat. Discard the parchment paper and spread the pecans in a single layer on the baking sheet to cool completely.

Raise the oven temperature to 450°F (230°C). Line a second rimmed baking sheet with parchment paper and coat generously with olive oil.

Cut the squash in half lengthwise and scrape out the seeds. Cut the flesh crosswise into slices 1 inch (2.5 cm) thick. Pile the squash on the prepared baking sheet. Drizzle with 2 tablespoons of the olive oil, season with salt and black pepper, and toss to coat. Spread the squash out in a single layer. Roast, turning several times, until fork-tender and lightly browned all over, about 25 minutes. Remove from the oven and cover with aluminum foil to keep warm.

In a bowl, whisk together the vinegar, mustard, and the remaining 2 tablespoons honey. Add the remaining 4 tablespoons (2 fl oz/60 ml) olive oil in a slow, steady stream, whisking constantly until emulsified. Season with salt and black pepper.

Transfer the endive to a large salad bowl. Pour in the dressing and toss to coat thoroughly. Add the warm squash, the pecans, and the dates. Toss to combine and serve.

Winter Greens, Roasted Pears & Pecorino

Kale, sorrel, and mizuna from local farmers' markets provide a good, pleasantly bitter mix to accompany the sweet roasted pear, but you can use any sturdy, cool-weather greens you like.

SERVES 4–6

½ cup (2½ oz/75 g) pine nuts

1 firm but ripe Bosc pear, halved and cored

1 tsp olive oil

¼ tsp salt

4 handfuls mixed winter greens, stems removed and leaves torn into bite-size pieces

½ cup (2 oz/60 g) coarsely grated pecorino cheese

2 Tbsp Champagne vinegar

½ tsp Dijon mustard

1 large shallot, finely chopped

¼ cup (2 fl oz/60 ml) nut oil such as walnut, almond, or pecan

Salt and freshly ground pepper

Preheat the oven to 375°F (190°C).

In a small, dry frying pan over medium heat, toast the pine nuts, stirring constantly, until fragrant and lightly browned, about 3 minutes. Remove from the heat and immediately transfer to a plate to cool. Set aside.

Cut each pear half into 6 thin wedges. In a bowl, toss the pear wedges with the olive oil and salt. Arrange the pears in a single layer in a baking pan or on a rimmed baking sheet and roast for 5 minutes. Remove from the oven and, using tongs, gently turn the pears. Return to the oven and roast until tender and slightly browned, 3–5 minutes longer. Let cool.

In a salad bowl, combine the greens, pine nuts, and cheese and toss to mix.

In a small bowl, whisk together the vinegar, mustard, and shallot. Add the nut oil in a slow, steady stream, whisking constantly until emulsified. Season with salt and pepper. Pour the dressing over the salad and toss to coat thoroughly. Top with the roasted pear slices, season with a few grinds of pepper, and serve.

great grains

Discovering the versatility
of grain salads can feel like
a revelation to hosts who've
never made them before.
They are ideal for rounding
out all sorts of menus, and
they perfectly showcase
nutrient-rich ingredients
like greens that make any
holiday meal more healthful.

Curried Grains with Cranberries, Kale & Pine Nuts

Grains have been a symbol of the autumn harvest for centuries, although modern-day cooks have only recently begun to reintroduce themselves to some of the lesser-known ancient varieties. An array of hearty grains—amaranth, quinoa, millet, barley, and bulgur—is available in well-stocked grocery stores. Here, several are combined in this appealing pilaf that's perfect for fall.

SERVES 6

1 Tbsp canola or vegetable oil

1 shallot, minced

1 clove garlic, minced

¼ cup (2 oz/60 g) basmati rice

¼ cup (2 oz/60 g) amaranth

¼ cup (1 oz/30 g) quinoa

¼ cup (2 oz/60 g) millet

2 cups (16 fl oz/500 ml) chicken broth

½ cup (2 oz/60 g) dried cranberries

1 Tbsp curry powder

Salt and freshly ground pepper

4–5 stalks lacinato kale, stems removed and leaves thinly sliced

½ cup (2½ oz/75 g) lightly toasted pine nuts

In a saucepan over medium-low heat, warm the oil. Add the shallot and garlic and sauté, stirring often, until tender, about 3 minutes. Add the rice, amaranth, quinoa, and millet. Increase the heat to medium and toast, stirring constantly, until the grains are fragrant and coated with the oil, 1–2 minutes. Add the broth, 1 cup (8 fl oz/250 ml) of water, cranberries, curry powder, ¾ teaspoon salt, and pepper to taste. Bring to a boil over high heat, reduce the heat to low, cover, and simmer until the grains are tender and the liquid is nearly absorbed, about 20 minutes.

Add the kale to the quinoa mixture. Cover and continue to cook until the kale is wilted and the grains are tender, about 5 minutes longer. Transfer to a serving bowl. Add the pine nuts and fluff with a fork to mix. Taste and adjust the seasonings. Transfer to a warmed serving dish and serve immediately.

Apple, Celery & Sourdough Bread Stuffing

The sourdough crust adds a pleasant chewiness to this moist, flavorful stuffing, but if you prefer a softer bite, you can trim it away. If you cannot find Granny Smiths, use another sweet-tart apple variety, such as Cameo, Jonagold, Cripps Pink, or Braeburn.

SERVES 8–10

¾ cup (6 oz/185 g) unsalted butter, plus more for greasing

1-lb (500-g) loaf sourdough bread, cut into ½-inch (12-mm) cubes with crust intact

2 large yellow onions, finely chopped

1½ cups (7½ oz/235 g) finely chopped celery, including some leaves

2 large Granny Smith apples, cored and diced

2 Tbsp chopped fresh sage, or 1 tsp dried sage

1 tsp dried thyme

½ tsp freshly grated nutmeg

Salt and freshly ground pepper

⅓ cup (½ oz/15 g) minced fresh flat-leaf parsley

3 large eggs, lightly beaten

2½ cups (20 fl oz/625 ml) turkey or chicken broth

Preheat the oven to 250°F (120°C). Lightly butter a 4-quart (4-l) baking dish.

Spread the bread cubes on 2 rimmed baking sheets and dry in the oven for 40 minutes. Remove from the oven and set aside. Raise the oven temperature to 375°F (190°C).

In a large frying pan over medium heat, melt 3 tablespoons of the butter. Add the onions and celery and sauté until soft, about 10 minutes. Transfer to a large bowl. In the same pan over medium heat, melt 2 tablespoons of the butter. Add the apples and sauté until glazed, about 5 minutes. Transfer to the bowl with the onion-celery mixture. Add the sage, thyme, and nutmeg, season with salt and pepper to taste, and mix well. In the same pan over medium heat, melt the remaining 7 tablespoons (3½ oz/105 g) butter. Add the bread cubes and parsley and toss to coat. Transfer to the bowl. In another bowl, combine the eggs and broth and whisk until blended. Pour the broth mixture over the bread mixture and toss gently.

Transfer the mixture to the prepared baking dish. Cover the dish with a buttered sheet of aluminum foil and bake for 20 minutes. Uncover and continue to bake until the top is golden brown and crisp, about 25 minutes longer. Let rest for about 10 minutes before serving.

Spicy Corn Bread Stuffing with Chorizo & Pepitas

Be sure to select Mexican-style fresh chorizo, not Spanish-style cured chorizo, for this bold-flavored stuffing. To save time on serving day, crumble the corn bread and dry it in the oven up to three days in advance, then keep it in an airtight container at room temperature.

SERVES 10–12

Butter for greasing

Buttermilk Corn Bread (page 248), cooled

5 Tbsp (3 fl oz/80 ml) extra-virgin olive oil

1 lb (500 g) Mexican-style fresh chorizo

1 yellow onion, diced

3 ribs celery, diced

1 large jalapeño chile, seeded and finely chopped

½ tsp ground cumin

¼ tsp chipotle chile powder

Salt and freshly ground pepper

2 Tbsp chopped fresh cilantro or flat-leaf parsley

3–4 cups (24–32 fl oz/750 ml–1 l) turkey or chicken broth, warmed

¼ cup (1 oz/30 g) toasted pepitas (pumpkin seeds)

Preheat the oven to 250°F (120°C). Butter a 9-by-13-inch (23-by-33-cm) baking dish.

Crumble the corn bread into large bite-size pieces with the crust intact (about 10 cups/1 lb/500 g). Spread the pieces and crumbs onto 2 rimmed baking sheets and dry in the oven for 45 minutes. Remove from the oven and set aside. Raise the oven temperature to 375°F (190°C).

In a frying pan over medium-high heat, warm 2 tablespoons of the oil. Add the chorizo and cook, breaking it up into small pieces with a spatula, until browned, about 6 minutes. Transfer the chorizo to paper towels to drain.

In the same pan over medium-high heat, warm the remaining 3 tablespoons oil. Add the onion, celery, jalapeño, cumin, chile powder, ¾ teaspoon salt, and a few grinds of pepper and sauté until the vegetables are soft, 8–10 minutes. Transfer the mixture to a large bowl and stir in the cilantro.

Add the corn bread and stir to mix. Stir in the broth ½ cup (4 fl oz/125 ml) at a time, making sure it is completely absorbed into the corn bread before adding more. Fold in the chorizo.

Transfer the mixture to the prepared baking dish. Sprinkle evenly with the pepitas. Cover the dish with a buttered sheet of aluminum foil and bake for 20 minutes. Uncover and continue to bake until the top is golden brown and crisp, about 25 minutes longer. Let rest for about 10 minutes before serving.

Brussels Sprouts with Currants & Shallots

With a little advance work, this dish will come together in no time, a boon when you're hosting a holiday dinner. Shave the Brussels sprouts and make the shallot-currant mixture up to 2 days in advance and refrigerate them. Just before serving, prepare the whole sprout leaves and then finish the dish.

SERVES 6–8

2 lb (1 kg) Brussels sprouts, trimmed

3 Tbsp dried currants

¼ cup (2 fl oz/60 ml) balsamic vinegar, warmed

3 Tbsp olive oil

½ lb (250 g) shallots, thinly sliced into rings

Salt and freshly ground pepper

Have ready a bowl of ice water. Bring a saucepan filled with water to a boil over high heat. Separate 10 Brussels sprouts into individual leaves. Add the leaves to the boiling water and cook until bright green, about 1 minute. Drain and plunge into the ice water to cool. Drain again, pat dry with paper towels, and set aside. Using a mandoline or the shredding blade of a food processor, thinly shave the remaining Brussels sprouts. Set aside.

In a small bowl, combine the currants and vinegar. Set aside.

In a large sauté pan over medium heat, warm 2 tablespoons of the olive oil. Add the shallots and sauté until softened and browned, about 15 minutes. Add the currants and vinegar and cook, stirring, until the liquid has evaporated, about 2 minutes. Transfer to a bowl.

In the same pan over medium heat, warm the remaining 1 tablespoon olive oil. Add the shaved Brussels sprouts and sauté until softened and beginning to brown, about 5 minutes. Return the shallot-currant mixture to the pan and stir until heated through, 1–2 minutes. Season to taste with salt and pepper. Place in a warmed serving dish. Sprinkle with the whole Brussels sprout leaves and serve.

Texture at The Table

A well-conceived menu offers not only the right balance of flavors but also a palate-pleasing combination of textures. Dishes like this one, which features both thinly shaved Brussels sprouts and whole leaves, create a study in contrasts that adds sophistication to any meal.

festive desserts

The holiday season calls for
homemade fruit desserts more
than any other time of the year.
Stay ahead of stress by creating a
timetable of tasks: while your pastry
dough rests, check your list and
tackle other hosting duties.

Apple-Cranberry Galettes

These beautiful open-faced pastries are a gorgeous finale for a holiday meal. Because the fruit filling has been simmered before it goes into the oven, the galettes bake quickly and evenly. Fresh thyme and a last-minute drizzle of honey offer an unexpected flavor nuance.

MAKES THREE 5-INCH (13-CM) GALETTES; SERVES 12

FOR THE PASTRY

1¾ cups (9 oz/280 g) all-purpose flour

6 Tbsp (2 oz/60 g) white cornmeal

2 tsp sugar

¾ tsp salt

¾ cup (6 oz/185 g) cold unsalted butter, cut into small pieces

6 Tbsp (3 oz/90 g) sour cream

½ cup (4 fl oz/125 ml) ice water

FOR THE FILLING

½ cup (4 oz/125 g) sugar

3 Tbsp honey

3 Tbsp fresh lemon juice

½ tsp ground cinnamon

8 large apples such as Golden Delicious or McIntosh or tart baking apple, about 4 lb (2 kg) total weight, peeled, cored, and sliced

1½ cups (6 oz/185 g) fresh cranberries

2 Tbsp unsalted butter, cut into thin slices

Crème fraîche (optional)

Thyme sprigs for garnish (optional)

Flaky sea salt for garnish (optional)

Honey for drizzling (optional)

To make the pastry, in a food processor, combine the flour, cornmeal, sugar, and salt. Scatter the butter pieces over the top and pulse for a few seconds until they are the size of small peas. In a small bowl, whisk together the sour cream and ice water, drizzle over the dough, and pulse until it is smooth and clings together. Flatten the dough into a disk, wrap in plastic wrap, and refrigerate for 20 minutes.

Meanwhile, to make the filling, in a large frying pan over medium heat, combine the sugar, ½ cup (4 fl oz/125 ml) water, the honey, lemon juice, and cinnamon and cook, stirring, until the sugar is dissolved. Stir in the apple slices and simmer until the apples begin to soften, 5–7 minutes. Using a slotted spoon, transfer the apple slices to a bowl. Add the cranberries to the frying pan and simmer until they start to pop, about 2 minutes. Using a slotted spoon, add the cranberries to the apples. Boil the liquid over medium-high heat until reduced slightly. Spoon over the fruit.

Position 2 racks in the middle of the oven and preheat to 400°F (200°C). Line a baking sheet with parchment paper.

Divide the dough into 3 equal pieces. On a lightly floured work surface, roll out each piece into a round about ⅛ inch (3 mm) thick, and transfer to the prepared baking sheet. Divide the filling equally between the pastry rounds and spread it in an even layer, leaving a 1½-inch (4-cm) border uncovered. Fold the border over the fruit, pleating the edges to form a rim. Lay the butter slices on the exposed fruit. Dust the pastry rims with sugar, if desired.

Bake the galettes, rotating them at the midway point, until the pastry is golden brown and the apples are tender, 35–40 minutes. Let cool completely on the pans on wire racks before serving. Serve with crème fraîche, if desired, and garnished with thyme sprigs, sea salt, or honey.

Bread Puddings with Caramel Sauce

These homey puddings are a welcome sight on nearly any casual fall or winter menu. You can refrigerate the unbaked ramekins for a few hours but no longer, as the pudding becomes soggier the longer it sits.

MAKES 6 PUDDINGS

4 Tbsp (2 oz/60 g) unsalted butter, melted, plus more for greasing

Granulated sugar

1 loaf challah, 1 lb (500 g), crust removed and bread torn into bite-sized pieces

1 cup (5 oz/155 g) finely chopped dried figs

1 cup (6 oz/185 g) finely chopped pitted dates

¼ cup (1½ oz/45 g) finely minced crystallized ginger

1 tsp ground cinnamon

¼ tsp ground allspice

5 large whole eggs, plus 2 large egg yolks

1 cup (7 oz/220 g) firmly packed dark brown sugar

3 cups (24 fl oz/750 ml) half-and-half

2 tsp vanilla extract

FOR THE CARAMEL SAUCE

½ cup (4 oz/125 g) sugar

1 Tbsp unsalted butter, cut into small pieces

¼ cup (2 fl oz/60 ml) heavy cream

Lightly butter six 1-cup (8–fl oz/250-ml) ramekins. Coat the bottom and sides with granulated sugar, tapping out the excess. In a large bowl, toss together the bread, figs, dates, ginger, cinnamon, allspice, and melted butter. In a separate bowl, whisk together the whole eggs, egg yolks, and brown sugar until blended and the sugar is dissolved, about 2 minutes. Stir in the half-and-half and vanilla. Pour the egg mixture into the bowl with the bread mixture and toss until well combined. Cover and refrigerate until most of the liquid is absorbed, about 1 hour.

Meanwhile, make the caramel sauce: Put the sugar in a heavy saucepan and add enough water just to cover (it will resemble wet sand). Place over medium-high heat and cook, swirling (not stirring) the pan occasionally to ensure even cooking, until the mixture starts to bubble and the edges begin to turn amber, 7–10 minutes. Watching carefully to prevent overcooking, heat until the mixture turns a deep amber, 3–5 minutes longer. Remove from the heat and very carefully add the butter (it may spatter) and then the cream, swirling the pan until the mixture is evenly blended. (You should have about ¾ cup/6 fl oz/180 ml.) Set the sauce aside until ready to serve, or store in an airtight container in the refrigerator for up to 3 days. Rewarm the sauce over low heat before serving.

Preheat the oven to 350°F (180°C). Divide the bread pudding mixture evenly among the prepared ramekins. Bake until the tops are golden and a toothpick inserted into the center of a pudding comes out clean, about 35 minutes. Transfer to a wire rack and let cool for 15 minutes.

Run a thin-bladed knife around the edge of each pudding to loosen it. Holding the ramekins with a kitchen towel to prevent burning yourself, remove each pudding from its ramekin and place it standing upright on a dessert plate. Pour caramel sauce over the top of each pudding and serve.

Special Occasion Cupcakes

When you want to serve a classic vanilla cupcake for dessert, these party-worthy cupcakes fit the bill. Top them according to whim or the celebration at hand, or try any of the variations below.

MAKES 12 CUPCAKES

1¼ cups (6¼ oz/200 g) all-purpose flour

1½ tsp baking powder

¼ tsp salt

¾ cup (6 oz/185 g) granulated sugar

6 Tbsp (3 oz/90 g) unsalted butter, at room temperature

1 large egg, plus 1 large egg white, at room temperature

1 tsp vanilla extract

½ cup (4 fl oz/125 ml) whole milk

FOR THE DARK CHOCOLATE FROSTING

½ lb (250 g) unsweetened chocolate, chopped

1 cup (8 oz/250 g) unsalted butter, at room temperature

2½ cups (10 oz/315 g) confectioners' sugar, sifted

2 tsp vanilla extract

decorations

FONDANT SHAPES Roll out tinted fondant, then cut into shapes.

CHOCOLATE SCRIPT Melt chocolate and spoon into a small plastic bag with a corner snipped. Pipe cursive letters onto wax paper. When the chocolate hardens, peel off the paper.

CHOCOLATE CURLS Warm a large bar of chocolate between your hands. Using a vegetable peeler, shave the chocolate into curls.

Position a rack in the middle of the oven and preheat the oven to 350°F (180°C). Line a standard 12-cup muffin pan with paper liners.

In a bowl, whisk the flour, baking powder, and salt. In a large bowl using an electric mixer on medium-high speed, beat the granulated sugar and butter together until light and fluffy, 2–3 minutes. Add the egg and egg white one at a time, beating well on low speed after each addition, then beat in the vanilla. Add the flour mixture in 3 additions, alternating with the milk in 2 additions, beating on low speed until just combined. Stop the mixer and scrape down the sides of the bowl as needed. Beat on medium-high speed just until no traces of flour remain, about 30 seconds; do not overbeat.

Divide the batter evenly among the prepared muffin cups, filling each cup about three-fourths full. Bake until lightly golden and a toothpick inserted into the center of a cupcake comes out clean, 18–20 minutes. Let the cupcakes cool in the pan on a wire rack for 5 minutes. Transfer the cupcakes to the wire rack and let cool.

Meanwhile, make the frosting: Put the chocolate in a small bowl and place over (not touching) barely simmering water in a pan. Warm, stirring often, until melted. Remove the bowl from over the water and let the chocolate cool. In the bowl of a stand mixer fitted with the paddle attachment, beat the butter and confectioners' sugar on medium speed until light and fluffy, about 3 minutes. Beat in the vanilla. Add the cooled chocolate and beat on low speed until incorporated, then increase the speed and beat until light and fluffy, about 2 minutes.

Frost the cooled cupcakes, then decorate as desired. (See note at left.)

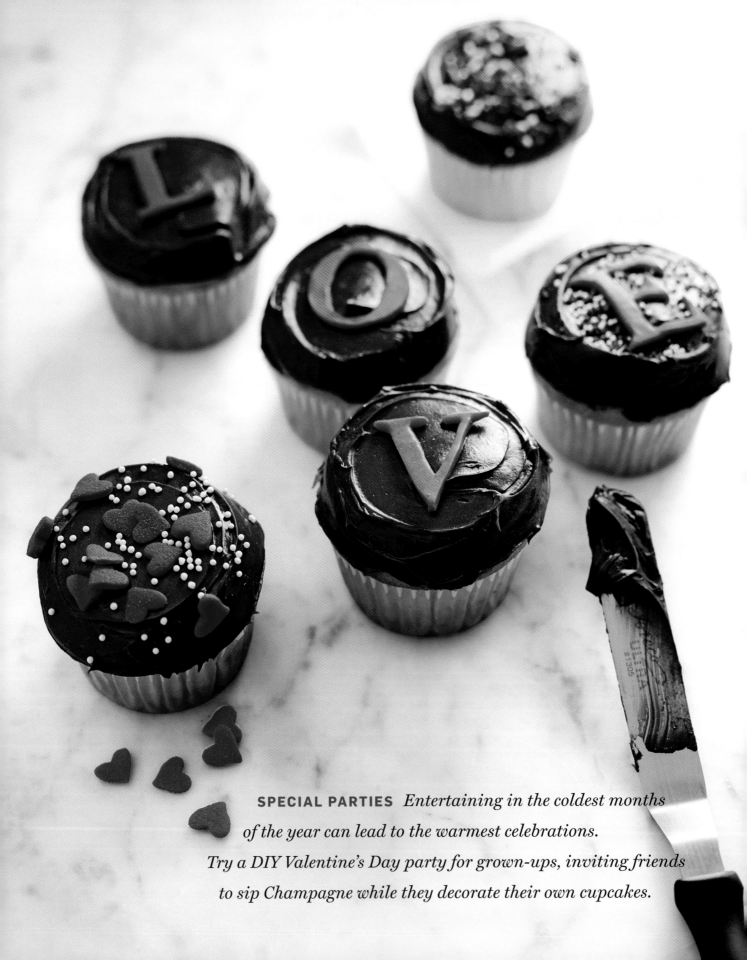

SPECIAL PARTIES *Entertaining in the coldest months of the year can lead to the warmest celebrations. Try a DIY Valentine's Day party for grown-ups, inviting friends to sip Champagne while they decorate their own cupcakes.*

A little frivolity goes a long way to making occasions memorable. From bright cupcake decorations to splashy cocktail garnishes, don't skimp on the little things that add quirkiness and fun to festive celebrations.

Spiced Ginger Bundt Cake

This richly spiced cake is ideally served warm, but that's often difficult to pull off as part of a multicourse holiday dinner. Fortunately, it is also good at room temperature. Drizzle the warm cake with caramel sauce, or top with spiced whipped cream, or both.

SERVES 12–16

1 cup (8 oz/250 g) unsalted butter, at room temperature, plus more for greasing

3 cups (15 oz/470 g) all-purpose flour, plus more for dusting

½ tsp salt

1 tsp baking soda

1 tsp ground cinnamon

1 tsp allspice

2 Tbsp ground ginger

¼ cup (1½ oz/45 g) peeled and grated fresh ginger

1 cup (7 oz/220 g) firmly packed light brown sugar

1 large egg

1 cup (11 oz/345 g) light molasses

1 cup (8 fl oz/250 ml) buttermilk

FOR THE NUTMEG WHIPPED CREAM (OPTIONAL)

1½ cups (12 fl oz/375 ml) heavy cream

6 Tbsp (1½ oz/45 g) confectioners' sugar

1 tsp freshly grated nutmeg, plus more for garnish

Caramel Sauce (page 208), warmed (optional)

Preheat the oven to 350°F (180°C). Butter a 10-inch (25-cm) Bundt pan or (12-cup) molded cake pan, including the tube. Dust lightly with flour and shake out any excess.

In a large bowl, whisk together the flour, salt, baking soda, cinnamon, allspice, ground ginger, and grated ginger. In another large bowl, using an electric mixer, beat together the butter and brown sugar until light and creamy. Beat in the egg. Add the molasses and beat until well blended, about 2 minutes. Beat in the flour mixture in 3 additions alternately with the buttermilk in 2 additions, beginning and ending with the flour mixture. Pour the batter into the prepared pan.

Bake until a toothpick inserted into the center of the cake comes out clean, about 50 minutes. Transfer to a wire rack and let cool in the pan for 10 minutes. Turn the cake out of the pan, slipping a knife between the edge of the cake and the pan to loosen. Turn the cake right side up and let cool for at least 15 minutes before serving.

Meanwhile, to make the whipped cream, if using: In a large bowl, using an electric mixer, beat the cream until soft peaks form. Sprinkle in the confectioners' sugar and 1 tablespoon nutmeg and continue to beat until almost stiff peaks form. Cover and refrigerate until ready to serve.

Drizzle the cake with the warm caramel sauce, if using, and cut into wedges. If desired, garnish each wedge with a dollop of whipped cream and sprinkle with nutmeg.

Pumpkin Pie
with Walnut Crust

*The walnut crust contributes both texture and flavor to this holiday
pie. Be sure to remove the pie from the oven when the filling is set
but the center still jiggles; if you overbake it, it will crack as it cools.*

SERVES 8

FOR THE PASTRY

1¼ cups (6½ oz/200 g) all-purpose flour

½ cup (2 oz/60 g) coarsely ground walnuts

2 Tbsp confectioners' sugar

¼ tsp salt

½ cup (4 oz/125 g) cold unsalted butter, cut into small pieces

2 Tbsp ice water

FOR THE FILLING

1¾ cups (14 oz/440 g) pumpkin purée

¾ cup (6 oz/185 g) granulated sugar

½ tsp salt

1 tsp ground cinnamon

½ tsp ground ginger

½ tsp freshly grated nutmeg

¼ tsp ground cloves

2 large eggs

1 cup (8 fl oz/250 ml) evaporated milk

Whipped cream or vanilla ice cream for serving (optional)

To make the pastry, in a food processor, combine the flour, walnuts, confectioners' sugar, and salt and pulse once or twice to blend. Add the butter pieces and pulse until the mixture is the size of small peas, about 45 seconds. With the machine running, add the ice water and process until the dough comes roughly together, adding up to 2 teaspoons more water if needed. Gather the dough into a ball, cover with plastic wrap, and flatten into a disk. Refrigerate overnight.

Bring the dough to room temperature 30–45 minutes before rolling it out. On a lightly floured work surface, roll out the disk into a round 12 inches (30 cm) in diameter and about ⁄₁₆ inch (2 mm) thick. Transfer the dough round to a 9-inch (23-cm) pie pan, gently patting it into the bottom and up the sides. Trim and crimp the edges.

Preheat the oven to 450°F (230°C).

To make the filling, in a large saucepan over medium heat, cook the pumpkin purée, stirring, until it begins to caramelize, about 5 minutes. Remove from the heat and stir in the granulated sugar, salt, cinnamon, ginger, nutmeg, and cloves. In a bowl, whisk together the eggs, evaporated milk, and ½ cup (4 fl oz/125 ml) water. Whisk the egg mixture into the pumpkin mixture.

Pour the filling into the pie shell. Bake the pie for 15 minutes. Reduce the oven temperature to 300°F (150°C) and continue to bake the pie until just the center jiggles when the pan is gently shaken, about 30 minutes longer. Transfer to a wire rack and let cool for at least 20 minutes.

Cut the pie into wedges. Serve warm or at room temperature accompanied by whipped cream or ice cream, if desired.

Apple-Ginger Tart with Cider-Bourbon Sauce

A warm bourbon sauce is the perfect addition to this streusel-topped apple tart. It can be made in advance and reheated over low heat just before serving. A pot of dark-roast coffee is an ideal accompaniment.

SERVES 8–10

FOR THE PASTRY

1¼ cups (6½ oz/200 g) all-purpose flour

⅔ cup (5 oz/155 g) cold unsalted butter

2 Tbsp confectioners' sugar

FOR THE FILLING

8 Granny Smith or Golden Delicious apples, about 3 lb (1.5 kg) total weight

⅓ cup (2½ oz/75 g) firmly packed light brown sugar

¼ cup (2 oz/60 g) granulated sugar

3 Tbsp fresh lemon juice

⅓ cup (2 oz/60 g) finely chopped crystallized ginger

1 tsp ground cinnamon

FOR THE CIDER-BOURBON SAUCE

1 cup (7 oz/220 g) firmly packed light brown sugar

2 Tbsp cornstarch

2 cups (16 fl oz/500 ml) apple cider

Pinch of salt

¼ cup (2 oz/60 g) unsalted butter

½ cup (4 fl oz/125 ml) bourbon

Preheat the oven to 425°F (220°C).

To make the pastry, in a food processor, combine the flour, butter, and confectioners' sugar. Pulse until fine crumbs form. Measure out ½ cup (2 oz/60 g) of the crumb mixture and set aside.

Pat the remaining crumb mixture evenly in the bottom and up the sides of an 11-inch (28-cm) tart pan with a removable bottom. Refrigerate or freeze the tart shell for 10 minutes. Bake until the crumb mixture just begins to brown, about 6 minutes. Let cool completely on a wire rack.

To make the filling, halve and core the unpeeled apples and then thinly slice. In a small bowl, mix together the reserved crumb mixture and the brown sugar. In a large bowl, combine the apple slices, granulated sugar, lemon juice, ginger, and cinnamon. Toss to coat the apples. Pile into the cooled pastry shell. Sprinkle with the crumb mixture.

Bake for 15 minutes. Lower the oven temperature to 375°F (190°C) and bake until the apples are tender when pierced with a knife, 45–50 minutes longer. Cover the top with aluminum foil during the last 30 minutes to prevent the top from overbrowning. Transfer to a wire rack and let cool.

To make the sauce, in a small saucepan over medium heat, combine the brown sugar and cornstarch, stirring to remove any lumps. Stir in the apple cider and salt. Raise the heat to medium-high and bring to a boil, stirring constantly. Cook until thickened, about 4 minutes. Lower the heat to medium, stir in the butter and bourbon, and simmer just until well blended.

Cut the tart into wedges. Drizzle a little of the hot cider-bourbon sauce over each wedge and serve.

Caramel-Nut Tart

Seek out fresh, high-quality nuts for this sweet, rich tart. It is delicious just as it is, but a dollop of vanilla ice cream or whipped cream on each slice is a nice addition. If you are pouring wine with dessert, look to a fortified type, such as tawny port or sherry.

SERVES 8–10

FOR THE PASTRY

1¼ cups (6½ oz/200 g) all-purpose flour

3 Tbsp granulated sugar

2 tsp grated lemon zest

½ cup (4 oz/125 g) cold unsalted butter, cut into small pieces, plus more for greasing

2 large egg yolks

2 tsp ice water

FOR THE FILLING

½ cup (4 oz/125 g) butter

½ cup (3½ oz/105 g) plus 2 Tbsp firmly packed dark brown sugar

¼ cup (3 oz/90 g) honey

1 cup (5½ oz/170 g) blanched whole almonds, toasted

1 cup (4 oz/125 g) walnuts, toasted

¾ cup (4 oz/125 g) salted roasted cashews

2 Tbsp heavy cream

To make the pastry, in a food processor, combine the flour, sugar, and lemon zest. Process to mix. Add the butter and pulse until the mixture resembles coarse meal. In a small bowl, whisk together the egg yolks and ice water until blended. Gradually pour into the flour mixture and process just until the dough begins to gather together. Form the dough into a ball and flatten into a disk. Wrap in plastic wrap and refrigerate for at least 30 minutes or up to 1 day.

Butter a tart pan 11 inches (28 cm) in diameter with a removable bottom. Roll the dough disk between sheets of waxed paper into a round ⅛ inch (3 mm) thick. Peel off the top sheet and transfer the round to the prepared pan. Peel off the remaining paper and press the pastry gently into the pan. Trim the edges even with the rim. Pierce the crust in a few places with a fork. Cover and freeze for at least 30 minutes or up to 3 days.

Preheat the oven to 400°F (200°C). Bake the crust until golden brown, about 18 minutes. Transfer to a wire rack to cool completely, then place on a baking sheet. Reduce the oven temperature to 350°F (180°C).

To make the filling, in a saucepan over low heat, combine the butter, brown sugar, and honey, and stir until the sugar is dissolved. Raise the heat to high and whisk until the mixture comes to a boil. Boil without stirring until large bubbles form, about 1 minute. Remove from the heat. Stir in the almonds, walnuts, cashews, and cream and immediately pour into the crust.

Bake until the filling bubbles, about 20 minutes. Transfer to the rack to cool for about 30 minutes. Remove the pan sides and let the tart cool completely. Place on a plate, cut into wedges, and serve.

dessert service

A wedge of pie on a paper plate is perfectly fine at a summer barbecue, but holidays call for more refinement. Create an elegant presentation and offer specialty teas, fortified wines, and/or espresso drinks alongside.

sweet endings

Nothing concludes a holiday
meal with more luxury than a
silky-smooth dessert made with
high-quality chocolate. It's the
perfect finish to bring everyone
back to the table for one final
indulgence and shared moment
together—even if they all insist
they can't eat one more bite.

Chocolate-Espresso Crèmes with Candied Orange Peel

For this remarkably easy and ultradecadent treat, use bittersweet chocolate containing at least 70 percent cacao. You can also flavor the whipped cream with a splash of vanilla extract. Use small dessert spoons or demitasse spoons for serving.

SERVES 6

2 cups (16 fl oz/500 ml) heavy cream

6 oz (185 g) bittersweet chocolate, finely chopped

1 Tbsp instant espresso powder

Cocoa powder for dusting

Candied orange peel (page 250) for garnish

In a large saucepan over medium-high heat, warm 1½ cups (12 fl oz/375 ml) of the cream until bubbles start to form on the surface. Remove from the heat and stir in the chocolate and espresso powder. Using a whisk, beat vigorously until the chocolate is melted and the mixture is silky smooth, about 1 minute. Divide the mixture evenly among 6 small ramekins or demitasse cups. Cover loosely with plastic wrap and refrigerate until well chilled and the edges are firm, at least 6 hours or up to 24 hours. Remove from the refrigerator 15 minutes before serving.

To serve, in a bowl, using an electric mixer or a whisk, whip the remaining ½ cup (4 fl oz/125 ml) cream until soft peaks form. Garnish each dessert with a dollop of whipped cream, a dusting of cocoa powder, and a few strips of orange peel.

CHAPTER FIVE

COCKTAIL PARTIES

Eat well, laugh often, love much

cocktail basics

Before the party, make sure your bar is stocked
with all the key tools: assorted glasses, a shaker
and a mixing glass, a bar spoon and a strainer,
a jigger and a channel knife. Have extra-large
ice cubes for drinks on the rocks, and don't
forget to garnish—those are the touches that will
make cocktail hour at your place feel special.

cosmopolitan

*moscow
mule*

*cherry
rum punch*

east side negroni

Cosmopolitan

SERVES 4

Ice cubes

2 oz (60 ml) citrus vodka

½ oz (15 ml) triple sec or cointreau

½ oz (15 ml) cranberry juice

½ oz (15 ml) fresh lime juice

Garnish such as fresh currant sprig
or lime twist

Fill a tall cocktail shaker half full with ice. Pour in the vodka, triple sec, cranberry juice, and lime juice. Cover and shake vigorously for 20 seconds, then strain into martini glasses. Garnish each glass and serve.

Old-Fashioned

SERVES 1

3 dashes Angostura bitters

1 orange slice

1 lemon wedge

1 maraschino cherry

1 sugar cube

Ice cubes

2½ fl oz (70 ml) blended Canadian whisky

In an old-fashioned glass, combine the bitters, orange slice, lemon wedge, cherry, and sugar cube. Using a cocktail muddler or the end of a wooden spoon, pulverize the ingredients in the bottom of the glass. Fill the glass with ice, add the whisky, stir well, and serve.

Cherry Rum Punch

SERVES 1

2 sweet cherries such as Bing or Rainier, pitted

1-inch (2.5-cm) chunk pineapple

1 tsp superfine sugar

2 fl oz (60 ml) light rum

2 fl oz (60 ml) fresh orange juice

1 fl oz (30 ml) fresh lime juice

1 dash bitters

Crushed ice

In a cocktail shaker, combine the cherries, pineapple, and sugar. Using a cocktail muddler or the end of a wooden spoon, pulverize the ingredients in the bottom of the shaker. Add the rum, orange juice, lime juice, and bitters. Cover and shake vigorously. Fill a glass with crushed ice, strain the punch into the glass, and serve.

Moscow Mule

Created in the 1940s as a way to sell vodka, Moscow Mules remain popular decades later. To be true to the drink's origin, prepare and serve it in a copper mug. Don't be tempted to replace the ginger beer with ginger ale—the cocktail will lose its kick and taste watered down.

SERVES 1

1½ oz (45 ml) Russian vodka

3½ oz (100 ml) ginger beer

1 oz (30 ml) lime juice

Crushed ice

Fresh mint leaves, for garnish

Pour the vodka, ginger beer, and lime juice into a copper mug or a highball glass. Add ice and stir well. Garnish with a mint leaf, if using, and serve.

East Side Negroni

This vodka-based riff on a classic Negroni combines both floral and earthy notes with orange-flower water and Grand Marnier. The delicate flavor nuance is sophisticated enough for New York's Upper East Side. Serve it on the rocks or straight up in a stemmed glass.

SERVES 1

Ice cubes

1½ oz vodka

¾ oz (20 ml) Campari

¾ oz (20 ml) sweet vermouth

3 or 4 drops orange flower water

¼ oz Grand Marnier or other orange liqueur

1 orange twist

Fill a cocktail shaker with ice. Add the vodka, Campari, vermouth, orange-flower water, and Grand Marnier. Cover and shake vigorously. Strain into a martini glass. Garnish with the orange twist and serve.

Pitcher Martinis

Whether the perfect martini should be shaken or stirred is a subject of great controversy, although the stirred rendition certainly makes more sense when serving a crowd. Mix the drink in a tall glass pitcher, then pour into martini glasses when guests arrive.

MAKES 1 QUART (32 FL OZ/1 L); SERVES 8–10

2½ cups (20 fl oz/625 ml) gin

¾ cup (6 fl oz/180 ml) dry vermouth

¾ cup (6 fl oz/180 ml) bottled or filtered water (not mineral water)

Lemon twists, olives, and cocktail onions (optional)

Pour the gin, vermouth, and water into a tall pitcher and chill well. To serve, pour into individual martini glasses and garnish as desired.

Dark & Stormy

This popular, Bermuda-born cocktail is a celebrated mix of dark (dark rum) and stormy (ginger beer). It is traditionally made with Gosling's Black Seal rum and Barritt's spicy ginger beer, but any variety of the same two components will yield similar results.

SERVES 1

Crushed ice or ice cubes

2 fl oz (60 ml) dark rum

6 fl oz (180 ml) ginger beer

1 lime wedge

Fill a highball glass with ice. Pour in the rum and then the ginger beer. Stir gently. Garnish with the lime wedge and serve.

Artisanal Cocktails

Modern mixologists create sophisticated drinks with top-shelf spirits, specialty liqueurs, freshly squeezed juices, and classy garnishes. With these no-fail recipes, you'll quickly master the art of making equally memorable cocktails at home.

Sparkling Brew

¼ fl oz (7 ml) St-Germain
Sparkling wine, chilled
Belgian-style ale fermented with berries
Blackberries

Pour the St-Germain into a coupe glass. Fill halfway with sparkling wine. Top off with the ale, garnish with blackberries, and serve.

SERVES 1

Sakerinha

1 lime, cut into 8 wedges
2 tsp superfine sugar, or to taste
Crushed ice
3 fl oz (90 ml) sake

Combine the lime wedges and
sugar in an old-fashioned glass.
Using a cocktail muddler or the
end of a wooden spoon, pulverize
the ingredients in the bottom of
the glass, pressing to extract as
much juice as possible from the
lime wedges. Add a handful of
crushed ice and top off with the
sake. Stir well and serve.

SERVES 1

Pomegranate Gin Fizz

Ice cubes
½ fl oz (15 ml) fresh lemon juice (from
1 lemon)
2 fl oz (60 ml) gin
1 tsp superfine sugar
1 fl oz (30 ml) pomegranate juice
1 fl oz (30 ml) club soda
1 lemon slice
Pomegranate seeds (optional)

Add 2 or 3 ice cubes to a rocks glass.
Fill a cocktail shaker half full with ice
and add the lemon juice, gin, sugar,
and pomegranate juice. Cover, shake
vigorously, then strain into the glass. Add
the club soda and stir well. Garnish with
a lemon slice and pomegranate seeds, if
using, and serve.

SERVES 1

Passion Fruit Caipirinha

1 lime
2 tsp superfine sugar
1 passion fruit, halved
2 fl oz (60 ml) cachaça
Ice cubes

On a work surface, firmly press and
roll the lime to release its juice and the
essential oils in its rind. Cut into 8 slices,
then halve each slice. Place the pieces
in an old-fashioned glass. Sprinkle with
sugar and crush with a cocktail muddler
or the end of a wooden spoon. Scoop the
flesh from the passion fruit halves into
the glass, add cachaça, and stir to mix.
Add ice and serve.

SERVES 1

MAKING MEMORIES *Be there for the special moments of your gathering. If you juice the citrus, fill the ice bucket, and ready the glassware ahead of time, you'll be part of the celebration instead of still rushing around to finish up long after the doorbell rings.*

Bar Snacks

Set out bowls of salty nibbles when you're serving drinks. Gourmet food stores have lots of options, but nothing beats one of these homemade snacks.

chickpeas + ground seeds

¼ tsp cumin seeds • ¼ tsp fennel seeds • ¼ tsp nigella seeds • ¼ tsp yellow mustard seeds • Pinch of fenugreek seeds • ½ tsp sea salt • ⅛ tsp cayenne pepper • 1 can (15 oz/470 g) chickpeas, drained and rinsed • ½ cup (4 fl oz/125 ml) canola oil

In a small, dry sauté pan over medium-low heat, combine the cumin, fennel, nigella, mustard, and fenugreek seeds and toast, stirring frequently, until fragrant, about 3 minutes. Pour the spices onto a small plate to cool, then transfer to a spice grinder or mortar and grind to a fine powder. Stir in the salt and cayenne. Set aside.

Pat the chickpeas dry with paper towels. Line a plate with a paper towel. In a large sauté pan over medium-high heat, warm the oil until shimmering. Gently add the chickpeas and fry, stirring frequently, until light brown and crisp, about 8 minutes. Using a slotted spoon, transfer the chickpeas to the paper towels to drain.

Sprinkle the chickpeas with the spice mixture and serve.

SERVES 4–6

popcorn + lemon butter

4 Tbsp (2 oz/60 g) unsalted butter • 1½ tsp finely chopped fresh thyme leaves • 1½ tsp fresh lemon juice • 1 tsp maple syrup • 1 tsp grated lemon zest • 2 Tbsp olive oil • ½ cup (3 oz/90 g) popcorn kernels • Flaky sea salt such as Maldon

In a small saucepan over medium heat, melt the butter. Add the thyme, lemon juice, maple syrup, and lemon zest and stir to mix well. Remove from the heat and cover to keep warm.

In a large, heavy-bottomed pot with a tight-fitting lid over medium-high heat, warm the olive oil. When the oil is shimmering, add the popcorn and immediately cover the pot. After the first kernels pop, cook, shaking occasionally, until all of the kernels have popped, about 4 minutes. Pour the popcorn into a large bowl.

Pour the warm flavored butter over the popcorn and toss to coat well. Season with flaky salt and serve.

SERVES 4–6

sweet potatoes + flaked salt

2 Tbsp olive oil, plus more for greasing • 1 lb (500 g) sweet potatoes, peeled, halved lengthwise, and cut crosswise into very thin slices
Flaky sea salt such as Maldon

Preheat the oven to 500°F (260°C). Lightly oil 2 baking sheets. Arrange the sweet potato slices in a single layer on the prepared sheets and drizzle with the oil. Bake until the slices are golden and crisp, about 10 minutes. Turn the slices, rotate the pans, and cook until the slices are golden and crisp on the second side, about 10 minutes longer. Transfer to paper towels to drain. Season with flaky salt and let stand at room temperature for 5 minutes. Transfer to a bowl and serve.

SERVES 4–6

mixed nuts + ground spices

1 lb (500 g) mixed shelled nuts such as almonds, walnuts, cashews, and pistachios • 2 Tbsp olive oil • 1 Tbsp sea salt
1 tsp sugar • 2 tsp sweet paprika • ½ tsp cayenne pepper

Preheat the oven to 350°F (180°C). In a bowl, combine the nuts, oil, salt, sugar, paprika, and cayenne and mix well. Spread the nuts in a single layer on a rimmed baking sheet. Toast, stirring several times, until the nuts are fragrant and have taken on color, about 10 minutes. Transfer to paper towels and let cool. Pour into a bowl and serve.

SERVES 8–10

Smoky Eggplant Dip

The key to achieving a great smoky flavor in this dip is to blacken and blister the eggplant skins fully. If you find a few dense seed pockets in the flesh, carefully scoop them out and discard them. Serve the dip with pita bread triangles or other flatbread or crudités.

MAKES ABOUT 2½ CUPS (20 OZ/625 G)

2 eggplants, 1 lb (500 g) total weight

Juice of 1 lemon

¼ cup (2 fl oz/60 g) extra-virgin olive oil

1 tsp minced garlic

½ tsp red pepper flakes

Salt and freshly ground black pepper

¼ cup (1¼ oz/35 g) crumbled feta cheese

1 Tbsp chopped fresh flat-leaf parsley

Preheat the oven to 500°F (260°C). Pierce the eggplants in several places. Roast, turning occasionally, until they collapse and the skin blackens, 15–30 minutes, depending on size. Remove from the oven and let cool.

When cool enough to handle, halve and scoop out the flesh, discarding the skin. Finely mince the flesh and transfer to a bowl. Add the lemon juice, olive oil, garlic, and red pepper flakes and stir until blended. Season to taste with salt and pepper.

Transfer to a food processor. Process until very smooth, adding a few teaspoonfuls of water or olive oil if needed to achieve a dip consistency. Taste and adjust the seasonings. Transfer to a serving dish, sprinkle with the feta and parsley, and serve.

Tiny Cheese Popovers

Most popover recipes call for pricking them the moment they emerge from the oven so they don't become soggy. But you can skip that step with these light, airy puffs. To make them in advance, leave them at room temperature then reheat before serving.

MAKES 24 MINI POPOVERS

Vegetable oil for greasing

1 cup (5 oz/155 g) all-purpose flour

½ tsp salt

¼ tsp freshly ground white pepper

1 Tbsp finely chopped fresh flat-leaf parsley

1¼ cups (10 fl oz/310 ml) milk, at room temperature

2 large eggs, at room temperature

1 Tbsp unsalted butter, melted

3 oz (90 g) Roquefort or other strong-flavored blue cheese, crumbled

Position a rack in the bottom third of the oven and preheat to 450°F (220°C). Generously oil two 12-cup nonstick mini popover or muffin pans with vegetable oil.

In a large bowl, whisk together the flour, salt, white pepper, and parsley. In a large measuring pitcher, whisk together the milk, eggs, and melted butter. Pour the wet ingredients over the dry ingredients and whisk together until just combined (it's okay if a few lumps remain). Pour the batter into the prepared popover cups to within about ¼ inch (6 mm) of the rim. Place a scant teaspoon of crumbled cheese in the center of each filled cup.

Bake for 10 minutes without opening the oven door. Reduce the heat to 350°F (180°C) and continue to bake until brown and crusty and fully puffed, 8–10 minutes longer.

Remove from the oven, immediately transfer to a warmed platter or napkin-lined bowl, and serve. Or let cool on racks for up to 2 hours, then reheat in a 350°F (180°C) oven for 10 minutes.

satisfying snacks

Cocktail party fare is generally built around finger food, but that doesn't mean it can't be satisfying. This beautiful hors d'oeuvre has the complex flavor of a sit-down supper dish.

Beef & Asparagus Negimaki

Japanese cooks wrap tender beef around green onions to make bite-size rolls called negimaki. In this riff on the classic, green onions are replaced with pencil-thin asparagus. Serve them as single spears, as here, or wrap each spear more completely in the meat and brown evenly, then cut the spears crosswise into pieces and serve like pieces of sushi.

SERVES 6–8

1 boneless sirloin steak, about 1½ lb (24 oz/750 g) and 1½ inches (4 cm) thick

24 thin asparagus, about 1 lb (500 g), tough ends removed

1 Tbsp canola oil

¼ cup (2 fl oz/60 ml) soy sauce, preferably low-sodium

¼ cup (2 fl oz/60 ml) sake

2 Tbsp turbinado sugar

Wrap the steak in plastic wrap and freeze for 20 minutes to make it easier to slice. Holding a long, thin knife at a 45-degree angle, slice the meat thinly across the grain into 24 slices, each ¼ inch (6 mm) thick. (Reserve any remaining steak for another use.)

Bring a large saucepan of salted water to a boil. Have ready a large bowl of ice water. Add the asparagus pieces to the boiling water and cook just until bright green but still firm, about 30 seconds. Drain and immediately transfer them to the ice water. Let stand until cool, about 2 minutes, then drain again and pat dry with paper towels. Set aside.

Lay a strip of steak on a work surface with a short end toward you. Center 1 asparagus piece across the meat and roll away from you, enclosing the asparagus in a tight roll. Secure with a toothpick. Repeat to make 24 rolls.

In a large frying pan over medium-high heat, warm the oil. Working in two batches, add the beef rolls, seam side down, and brown the bottoms, 1 minute. Turn to brown the rolls on all sides, 2–3 minutes longer. Transfer the rolls to a plate and set aside.

Add the soy sauce, sake, and sugar to the pan, stirring until the sugar is dissolved. Return all the beef rolls to the pan along with their accumulated juices and cook until the meat is tender, about 4 minutes. Using tongs, transfer the rolls to a serving platter.

Boil to reduce the pan liquid until syrupy, about 4 minutes. Brush the glaze evenly over the beef rolls and serve.

Lamb Meatballs in Lettuce Cups with Mint Yogurt

Serving these allspice-flavored meatballs in little romaine lettuce cups makes them both eye-appealing and easy to pick up and eat. To find well-shaped, small leaves, look for hearts of romaine. If pomegranates are in season, tear one open to show off its garnet seeds and place in the center of the platter. Guests can also snag a seed or two, if they like.

SERVES 6

½ cup (3 oz/90 g) bulgur wheat

Boiling water

½ cup (4 oz/125 g) plain yogurt

2 Tbsp chopped fresh mint, plus
2–3 Tbsp shredded fresh mint leaves

1 lb (500 g) ground lamb

¼ cup (1½ oz/45 g) minced yellow onion

2 Tbsp chopped fresh flat-leaf parsley

3 cloves garlic, minced

⅛ tsp ground allspice

Salt and freshly ground pepper

2 Tbsp olive oil

12 small romaine lettuce leaves

1 cup (6 oz/185 g) cherry or grape tomatoes, halved

½ cup (2½ oz/75 g) seeded and chopped cucumber

variation

Substitute crisp, salty pita chips for the romaine lettuce leaves and top with meatballs, dollops of the herbed yogurt, and a sprinkle of mint.

Put the bulgur in a heatproof bowl and pour in boiling water to cover. Set aside to soften, about 15 minutes.

Meanwhile, in another bowl, combine the yogurt and chopped mint and stir to mix well. Set the yogurt sauce aside.

Drain the bulgur in a fine-mesh sieve and press on it with the back of a spoon to remove as much liquid as possible. Transfer the bulgur to a large bowl.

Add the lamb, onion, parsley, garlic, and allspice to the bulgur, season with salt and pepper, and stir to mix thoroughly. Divide the mixture into 12 equal portions and shape each portion into a ball.

In a large frying pan over medium-high heat, warm the olive oil. Add the meatballs and cook, turning as needed, until browned all over but still pink in the center, about 5 minutes. Transfer the meatballs to paper towels to drain and let cool slightly.

To serve, spoon about 2 teaspoons of the yogurt sauce into each romaine leaf. Top each with a meatball, 1 or 2 tomato halves, and 2 teaspoons of the cucumber. Arrange the filled leaves on a large platter. Scatter the shredded mint over the top and serve.

Cherry Tomatoes Stuffed with Blue Cheese

No one can resist these summery small bites. Look for cherry tomatoes in a variety of colors—red, yellow, orange, green—for a showy presentation. To take the flavor in a different direction, trade out the blue cheese for fresh goat cheese and the green onion garnish for snipped fresh chives.

SERVES 10

¼ lb (125 g) blue cheese, at room temperature

3 oz (90 g) cream cheese, at room temperature

2 Tbsp sour cream

20 cherry tomatoes, halved through the stem end

Sliced green onions for garnish

In a food processor, combine the blue cheese, cream cheese, and sour cream. Process until smooth, scraping down the sides of the bowl as needed.

Using the smaller end of a melon baller or a teaspoon, carefully scoop out the seeds and central rib from each tomato half and place, cut sides up, on a plate. (At this point, the tomatoes and cheese mixture can be refrigerated for up to 2 hours.)

About 20 minutes before serving, using 2 small spoons, stuff about ¾ teaspoon of the blue cheese mixture into each tomato half, mounding it up over the rim. Arrange on a platter, garnish with green onions, and serve.

Crostini Four Ways

Each one of these seasonally-inspired toppings for crostini (page 248) makes enough for 6 to 8 toasts.

smoked salmon
+
cream cheese

8 oz (226 g) cream cheese • 3 oz (90 g) smoked salmon
½ tsp freshly ground pepper
1 lemon, thinly sliced, for garnish (optional)

Spread the cream cheese over the crostini. Cut the smoked salmon into 1½-inch (4-cm) pieces and top each crostini with a piece of salmon. Season with pepper and garnish with a lemon slice, if using.

tomato
+
basil
+
mozzarella

8 oz (250 g) fresh mozzarella cheese, sliced
About 2 cups (12 oz/375 g) cherry tomatoes, halved
Salt and freshly ground pepper
½ cup (½ oz/15 g) loosely packed basil leaves

Top each crostini with 1 or 2 slices of mozzarella. Arrange a few tomato halves on top of the mozzarella, and sprinkle with salt and pepper. Garnish with basil leaves.

ricotta
+
pea

1 cup (6½ oz/ 200 g) shelled peas • 1 cup (8 oz/250 g) whole-milk
ricotta cheese, drained • 8 large or 24 small radishes, trimmed and
thinly sliced • Olive oil for drizzling • Salt and freshly ground pepper
Pea shoots for garnish (optional)

Blanch the peas (see page 39). Spread the ricotta on the crostini
then top each with some blanched peas and a few radish slices.
Drizzle with olive oil, sprinkle with salt and pepper, then garnish
with the pea shoots, if using.

gorgonzola
+
cherry
+
apple

8 oz (250 g) Gorgonzola cheese, sliced • 4 sweet apples,
such as Braeburn, Gala, or Red Delicious, thinly sliced
2 cups (8 oz/500 g) cherries, pitted and halved
Honey for drizzling

Top each crostini with 2 slices of Gorgonzola cheese,
a few slices of apple, and a few cherry halves. Drizzle
with honey.

Crispy Five-Spice Calamari with Lime

Chinese five-spice is also known as five-fragrance powder and five heavenly spices. It is indeed heavenly: sweet, sour, bitter, and pungent, all in one blend. Keep the presentation casual—pile the calamari onto a board with the sauce in a bowl alongside. Guests can pick up the tasty morsels with their fingers and dunk them in the sauce—napkins optional.

SERVES 4–6

FOR THE DIPPING SAUCE

2 Tbsp Asian sesame oil

2 Tbsp honey

2 Tbsp chopped peanuts

1 Tbsp chopped fresh cilantro

1 Tbsp rice vinegar

1 Tbsp fish sauce

1 Tbsp fresh lime juice

2 tsp soy sauce

1 small shallot, coarsely chopped

¼ tsp Chinese five-spice powder

1 lb (500 g) cleaned squid tentacles and bodies, thawed if frozen

1 cup (8 fl oz/250 ml) buttermilk

¼ cup (1½ oz/45 g) white rice flour

1 Tbsp Chinese five-spice powder

Salt

Rice bran oil or grapeseed oil for deep-frying

Lime or lemon wedges

To make the dipping sauce, in a blender or food processor, combine the sesame oil, honey, peanuts, cilantro, vinegar, fish sauce, lime juice, soy sauce, shallot, and five-spice powder and process until smooth. Taste and adjust the seasoning. Pour into a small serving bowl and set aside.

Rinse the squid and pat dry. Cut the bodies crosswise into rings about ⅓ inch (9 mm) wide. Leave the tentacles whole. In a large bowl, combine the squid and buttermilk and toss to coat well. In a shallow bowl, whisk together the rice flour, five-spice powder, and ½ teaspoon salt. Have ready a colander or medium-mesh sieve set atop another large bowl.

In a deep fryer or large, heavy pot (preferably cast iron), pour the oil to a depth of 2–3 inches (5–7.5 cm) and heat to 370°F (188°C) on a deep-frying thermometer.

Working in batches, and using a slotted spoon, transfer the squid to the seasoned flour and toss to coat evenly, and then to the colander to shake off any excess flour. Still using the spoon, carefully lower the squid, a few pieces at a time, into the hot oil. Fry until golden brown and crisp, 1–2 minutes. Place on paper towels to drain and sprinkle with salt. Repeat with the remaining squid. Serve with the lime wedges and dipping sauce.

Tuna Tartare on Wonton Crisps

Don't shy away from preparing raw fish. Go to a fish market that carries sushi-grade tuna and work quickly when you are cutting the fish, and this dish will be a success. The Asian flavors of ginger, soy, chile, and lime juice highlight the clean, silky taste of the tuna, and a scattering of sesame seeds delivers a nice crunch.

SERVES 8-12

FOR THE WONTON CRISPS

12 wonton wrappers, halved diagonally

Asian sesame oil for brushing

1 Tbsp black or white sesame seeds

2 tsp sesame seeds

1 lb (500 g) sushi-grade tuna fillet, well chilled

1½ Tbsp soy sauce, preferably low-sodium

1½ Tbsp Asian sesame oil

2¼ tsp fresh lime juice

1 jalapeño chile, finely minced

¾ tsp peeled and minced fresh ginger

1 Tbsp snipped chives

To make the wonton crisps, preheat the oven to 350°F (180°C). Line a baking sheet with parchment paper. Arrange the wonton triangles in a single layer on the prepared baking sheet, brush lightly with sesame oil, and sprinkle with the sesame seeds. Bake until crisp and golden, 6 to 8 minutes. Let cool.

In a small, dry frying pan over medium heat, toast the 2 teaspoons sesame seeds, stirring often, until fragrant and beginning to brown, 2–5 minutes. Pour onto a small plate to cool.

Using a very sharp knife, trim away any sinew or skin from the tuna fillet. Cut the tuna into ¼-inch (6-mm) cubes and place in a bowl. Add the soy sauce, sesame oil, lime juice, jalapeño, and ginger and stir gently to combine. Use at once or cover and refrigerate for up to 1 hour.

To serve, divide the tuna equally among the wonton crisps and sprinkle evenly with the chives and toasted sesame seeds.

Fresh Canapés

The key to creating tasty canapés has more to do with a willingness to experiment than expert knowledge or refined ingredients. Go for an inspired blend of tastes, textures, and colors—balancing salty and sweet, light and rich, fruity and creamy, and soft and crunchy.

SERVES A CROWD

FOR FRUIT BASES
Small stone fruit halves; large stone fruit wedges; fig halves; slit pitted dates; sliced melon cut-outs; apple and pear slices

FOR VEGETABLE BASES
Cucumber slices; pickle slices; watermelon radish slices or small radish halves; radicchio leaves; endive leaves; carrot slices; cherry tomato halves; small roasted potato halves; zucchini and summer squash slices; baby bell pepper halves; mushroom caps

FOR CHEESE TOPPINGS
Choose a mix of fresh and aged cheeses in a variety of textures: hard (Parmesan, dry Jack, aged Gouda), shaved or cut into small chunks; semi-hard (Gouda, Gruyère, Cheddar), shaved; semi-soft (blue, Roquefort, havarti), thinly sliced; soft (Brie, fresh goat, fresh mozzarella, burrata), thinly sliced

FOR CHARCUTERIE TOPPINGS
Choose a mix of cured meats: salami; prosciutto; mortadella; bresaola; speck; soppressata; smoked ham; rillettes; fried bacon, crumbled

FOR GARNISHES
Fresh herbs (leaves or sprigs); edible blossoms; nuts, halves or coarsely chopped; pitted olives, chopped or halved; sun-dried tomatoes, chopped or slivered; cornichons; mushrooms, sliced; tobiko or caviar; dried fruit, chopped; pomegranate seeds; berries; citrus segments or zest; honeycomb or honey drizzle

EXPERIMENT with different flavor combinations. For the canapés at right, pair the following (from top):

peach wedges + basil leaves + sliced prosciutto

fig halves + Gorgonzola + honeycomb + chopped hazelnuts

apricot halves + goat cheese + tarragon + cracked pepper

plum halves + sliced Brie + pomegranate seeds

lemon cucumber slices + feta + pitted olive halves + cherry tomato slices + fresh herbs

radish halves + ash-coated goat cheese + fresh thyme sprigs

MORE COMBINATIONS TO TRY:

watermelon cut-outs + feta + pine nuts

cherry tomato halves + bocconcini + fresh basil

slit pitted dates + Manchego + marcona almonds

small roasted potato halves + goat cheese + caviar

apple slices + Cheddar + fried bacon

mushroom caps + Gouda chunks + bresaola

baby bell pepper halves + burrata + sliced olives

pitted cherry halves + Roquefort + lemon zest

large radish slices + Gruyère cheese + chopped walnuts

cucumber slices + rillettes + sun-dried tomatoes

melon cut-outs + Brie + proscuitto

fig halves + fresh goat cheese + speck

simple pairings

Combine seasonal produce with cheese and/or charcuterie to delight cocktail party guests with colorful bite-size appetizers that carry more appeal and flavor than the typical array of cheese and crackers. Arrange favorite pairings on a platter, then let guests help themselves.

Menus

Settling on a menu for your gathering doesn't have to be complicated if you allow the mood and type of occasion guide you. Above all, remember that relying on good-quality seasonal ingredients is the single best way to ensure everything you make tastes fresh and delicious.

Winter Holiday Breakfast

Bellinis (page 44)

Cranberry Magic (page 44)

Baked Eggs with Spinach & Cream (page 40)

Baked Apples with Dried Fruit
& Honey Glaze (page 43)

Cinnamon-Nutmeg Baked French Toast (page 30)

Lazy Weekend Brunch

Spicy Bloody Marys (page 45)

Leeks, Pancetta & Gruyère Pastry Toasts (page 38)

Warm Kale Salad with Crispy Bacon
& Egg (page 124)

Roasted Plums with Honey-Vanilla Yogurt (page 155)

Caramel-Pecan Sticky Buns (page 32)

Easter Brunch Buffet

Perfect Ramos Fizz (page 45)

Springtime Frittata (page 29)

Caramel-Pecan Sticky Buns (page 32)

Baked Ham with Spiced Cider Glaze (page 191)

Honey-Balsamic Roasted Carrots (page 152)

Super Bowl Party

Popcorn with Lemon Butter (page 230)

Sweet Potato Chips with Guacamole
(pages 231 and 72)

Serve-Yourself Chili con Carne (page 49)

DIY Panini Press Cubanos (page 48)

Chocolate-Flecked Mint Ice Cream
Sandwiches (page 99)

Valentine's Day Celebration

Fresh Canapés (page 242)

Asparagus with Parmesan Bread Crumbs (page 147)

Pan-Seared Lamb Chops with
Herb-Almond Pesto (page 193)

Soft Chocolate Mini Cakes (page 160)

L-O-V-E Cupcakes (page 209)

Cinco de Mayo

Plum & Apricot Sangria (page 88)

Watermelon & Feta Salad (page 62)

Jicama Slaw with Chile-Lime Dressing (page 75)

Fish Tacos with Grilled Pineapple Salsa (page 70)

Mango-Pistachio Ice Pops (page 100)

Lunch on the Patio

Sparkling Limeade (page 89)

Ricotta and Pea Crostini (page 239)

Simplest Gazpacho (page 54)

Steak Salad with Red Rice, Yellow Tomatoes
& Mango (page 51)

Strawberry-Hazelnut Shortcakes (page 103)

Outdoor Picnic

Roasted Baby Artichokes with Aioli (page 117)

Zucchini, Basil & Fontina Quichelets (page 36)

Quinoa with Roasted Vegetables
& Goat Cheese (page 46)

Tandoori-Style Chicken Kebabs (page 95)

Fruity Hand Pies (page 104)

ready to share
Welcome guests to your holiday table with a beautifully presented Cider-Brined Spice-Rubbed Turkey (recipe page 182).

Casual Summer Barbecue

Grilled Shishito Peppers with Sea Salt (page 57)

Grilled Figs with Prosciutto (page 60)

Summer Ceviche (page 63)

Marinated Steak with Corn, Arugula
& Tomato Salad (page 82)

Grilled Peaches with Cardamom Cream (page 102)

Make-Ahead Dinner Party

Citrus Salad with Mint & Marcona Almonds
(page 119)

Whole Roasted Fish Stuffed with
Fennel & Thyme (page 135)

Barley Pilaf with Chanterelles (page 144)

Haricots Verts with Crispy Shallots & Chiles (page 196)

Caramel Pots de Crèmes (page 158)

Late-Summer Dinner

Mai Tais (page 87)

Grilled Salt & Pepper Shrimp (page 116)

Grilled T-Bone Steak with
Grilled Scallions & Garlic Butter (page 131)

Roasted Tomatoes with Fresh Herbs (page 150)

Pavlova with Summer Berries (page 163)

Autumn Dinner

Moscow Mules (page 224)

Warm Kale Salad with Crispy Bacon
& Egg (page 124)

Herb-Brined Pork Loin with
Apple-Ginger Compote (page 185)

Curried Grains with Cranberries,
Kale & Pine Nuts (page 201)

Caramel-Nut Tart (page 216)

Cozy Winter Dinner

Coconut-Curry Butternut Squash Soup (page 148)

Citrus Salad with Mint & Marcona Almonds (page 119)

Balsamic-Braised Beef Short Ribs (page 125)

Spicy Broccolini with Garlic (page 153)

Honey-Roasted Pears (page 154)

Thanksgiving Feast

Squash Soup with Thyme Cream (page 181)

Crottin Salad with Pears, Fennel
& Currants (page 178)

Maple-Mustard Turkey with
Cranberry Relish (page 184)

Apple, Celery & Sourdough Bread
Stuffing (page 202)

Pumpkin Pie with Walnut Crust (page 214)

Christmas Dinner

Roasted Parsnip & Apple Soup with
Gruyère Toasts (page 179)

Shaved Persimmon Salad with
Endive & Pomegranate (page 177)

Rib Roast with Horseradish Sauce (page 190)

Brussels Sprouts with Currants
& Shallots (page 204)

Spiced Ginger Bundt Cake (page 213)

Hanukkah Dinner

Potato-Apple Pancakes with Smoked Trout (page 170)

Zucchini, Basil & Fontina Quichelets (page 36)

Roast Chicken with Potatoes & Carrots (page 127)

Green Beans with Crispy Shallots (page 196)

Apple-Cranberry Galettes (page 207)

New Year's Cocktail Party

East Side Negronis (page 224)

Pitcher Martinis (page 225)

Tiny Cheese Popovers (page 233)

Beef & Asparagus Negimaki (page 235)

Smoked Salmon Crostini (page 238)

Midnight Supper

Elderflower Gin Fizz (page 121)

Oysters Mignonette (page 167)

Creamy Cauliflower Soup with
Crispy Prosciutto (page 149)

Roasted Lobster with Garlic-Lemon Butter (page 194)

Beignets with Dark Chocolate Sauce (page 159)

Tart Pastry

1 cup (5 oz/155 g) all-purpose flour

1 Tbsp sugar

½ tsp kosher salt

½ cup (4 oz/125 g) cold butter, cut into ½-inch (12-mm) pieces

½ tsp vanilla extract

In a bowl, stir together the flour, sugar, and salt. Work the butter into the flour mixture with your fingertips, pressing and blending until the butter looks granular and the mixture begins to hold together. Combine 1 tablespoon water and the vanilla and work it into the flour mixture with a fork until the ingredients are well combined and the pastry holds together when pressed. Gather the pastry dough into a ball and wrap it in plastic wrap.

Let the dough rest for 30 minutes to allow the flour to absorb the moisture. Then, use your fingertips to press the pastry into the bottom and sides of a 9-inch (23-cm) round or heart-shaped tart pan, making sure it is distributed evenly. Cover and place the tart shell in the freezer for 30 minutes to firm. Bake as directed in individual recipes.

MAKES ENOUGH FOR ONE 8- OR 9-INCH
(22- OR 23-CM) TART SHELL

Double-Crust Flaky Pie Dough

2 cups (10 oz/315 g) all-purpose flour

½ tsp kosher salt

1 tsp sugar (optional; omit if making a savory dish)

¾ cup (6 oz/185 g) very cold unsalted butter, cut into cubes

8 tbsp (4 fl oz/125 ml) ice water, plus more if needed

In the bowl of a food processor, mix the flour, salt, and sugar, if using. Sprinkle the butter over the top and pulse for a few seconds, or just until the butter is slightly broken up into the flour but still in visible pieces. Evenly sprinkle the water over the flour mixture, then process just until the mixture starts to come together. Dump the dough onto a work surface, press it together, then divide it in half. Press each half into a disk and wrap in plastic wrap. Refrigerate the dough for 30 minutes or up to 1 day, or freeze for up to 1 month.

MAKES ENOUGH FOR ONE 9-INCH (23-CM)
DOUBLE-CRUST PIE

Flatbread & Pizza Dough

1 cup (8 fl oz/250 ml) warm water (105°–115°F/40°–46°C)

1½ tsp active dry yeast

½ tsp sugar

2 cups (10 oz/315 g) all-purpose flour, plus more as needed

½ tsp salt

Olive oil for greasing

Pour the warm water into a large bowl. Sprinkle the yeast and sugar over the water. Let stand until the yeast is foamy, about 1 minute. Stir until the yeast dissolves.

Add the flour and salt to the yeast mixture and stir until a rough dough forms. Turn the dough out onto a lightly floured work surface and knead until smooth and elastic, about 10 minutes, dusting with more flour as needed. The dough should be soft but not sticky.

Lightly grease a large bowl with oil. Put the dough in the bowl and turn to coat with the oil. Cover the bowl with a kitchen towel, place in a warm, draft-free place, and let the dough rise until it doubles in size, about 1 hour.

Punch down the dough and turn out onto a lightly floured work surface. Press out all of the air bubbles, cover with a kitchen towel, and let rest for 10 minutes.

Shape and bake as directed in the individual recipes. (Or, if made ahead, place the dough in a resealable plastic bag and store in the refrigerator for up to 4 days or in the freezer for up to 1 month. Bring to room temperature before continuing.)

MAKES ENOUGH FOR 1 LARGE PIZZA OR FLATBREAD

Buttermilk Corn Bread

2 cups (14 oz/440 g) coarse-ground yellow cornmeal

1 cup (5 oz/155 g) all-purpose flour

⅓ cup (3 oz/90 g) sugar

4 tsp baking powder

1 tsp salt

1½ cups (12 fl oz/375 ml) buttermilk, at room temperature

2 large eggs, well beaten

½ cup (4 oz/125 g) unsalted butter, melted

Preheat the oven to 400°F (200°C). Grease a 9-by-13-inch (23-by-33-cm) baking pan.

In a large bowl, stir together the cornmeal, flour, sugar, baking powder, and salt, mixing well. In another bowl, stir together the buttermilk, eggs, and butter just until mixed. Stir the wet ingredients into the dry ingredients just until combined. Spread the batter in the prepared pan.

Bake until the edges of the corn bread are just beginning to pull away from the sides of the pan and a knife inserted into the center comes out clean, 18–20 minutes. Let stand in the pan for at least 5 minutes, then turn out onto a wire rack to cool. Cut into squares and serve.

SERVES 8-10

Crostini

1 French baguette, Italian Pugliese, or other favorite bread

2 Tbsp extra-virgin olive oil

Place an oven rack in the upper third of an oven and preheat the broiler, or prepare a charcoal or gas grill for direct heat cooking over high heat.

Cut the bread on the diagonal into slices ¼ inch (6 mm) thick. If broiling, arrange the slices on a baking sheet and drizzle with the olive oil. If grilling, brush the slices with the olive oil. Place the bread slices under the broiler or on the grill rack and toast, turning once, until golden brown on both sides, about 2 minutes per side. Remove from the heat and let cool, then top as directed in individual recipes.

MAKES 20–24 TOASTS

Saffron Aioli

½ cup (4 fl oz/125 ml) canola oil
¼ cup (2 fl oz/60 ml) extra-virgin olive oil
2 large egg yolks
1 Tbsp Dijon mustard
3 cloves garlic
¼ tsp saffron threads, finely chopped
½ tsp salt
¼ tsp ground white pepper
1–2 Tbsp fresh lemon juice

Combine the oils in a measuring cup with a spout. In a blender, combine the egg yolks, mustard, garlic, saffron, salt, and white pepper. Pulse several times until the garlic is pulverized. With the motor running, add the oils in a slow steady stream. Stir in 1 tablespoon of the lemon juice, adding more lemon juice if needed to thin the aioli; it should be the consistency of mayonnaise. Serve right away, or store in an airtight container in the refrigerator for up to 2 days.

MAKES 2 CUPS (1 LB/500 G)

Quick Pizza Sauce

1 Tbsp olive oil
¼ yellow onion, finely chopped
1 clove garlic, minced
1 can (28 oz/875 g) diced tomatoes with juices
1 Tbsp tomato paste
2 tsp minced fresh oregano or basil or ½ tsp dried oregano
Salt and freshly ground pepper

In a large saucepan over medium heat, warm the oil. Add the onion and sauté until tender and translucent, about 10 minutes. Add the garlic and sauté for 1 minute longer. Stir in the tomato, tomato paste, and oregano. Raise the heat to medium-high and cook, stirring occasionally to break up the tomatoes, until the excess moisture evaporates and the sauce is a good spreading consistency, 10–15 minutes. Season to taste with salt and pepper. Let cool to lukewarm before spreading on pizza dough, or let cool to room temperature and store in an airtight container in the refrigerator for up to 3 days.

MAKES 2½ CUPS (20 FL OZ/625 ML)

Classic BBQ Sauce

1 cup (8 oz/250 g) ketchup
2 Tbsp yellow mustard
1 Tbsp cider vinegar
2 tsp firmly packed dark brown sugar
½ cup (4 fl oz/125 ml) low-sodium chicken broth
Salt and freshly ground pepper

In a saucepan over medium heat, combine the ketchup, mustard, vinegar, sugar, broth, a pinch of salt, and 2 teaspoons pepper and bring to a simmer, stirring to dissolve the sugar. Simmer for 5 minutes for a relatively thin sauce or for 10–15 minutes for a thick sauce. Taste and adjust the seasoning with salt. Use right away, or let cool and store in an airtight container in the refrigerator for up to 1 month.

MAKES 2½ CUPS (20 FL OZ/625 ML)

Spiced Stone Fruit Chutney

2 lb (1 kg) yellow peaches
1 mango, peeled and pitted
½ cup (6 oz/185 g) diced fresh or canned pineapple
3 Tbsp light agave syrup
2 Tbsp cider vinegar
2 Tbsp lightly packed golden brown sugar
½ tsp *each* ground cinnamon and ground cardamom
2 dashes Tabasco or other hot pepper sauce, or to taste

Pit the peaches and mango and cut each into ½-inch (12-mm) dice. In a heavy saucepan over medium-high heat, combine the peaches, mango, pineapple, agave syrup, vinegar, brown sugar, cinnamon, cardamom, and hot pepper sauce and bring to a boil. Reduce the heat to medium and cook the chutney, stirring well, until syrupy and thick and the fruit softens, 5–6 minutes. Let cool. Serve right away, or store in an airtight container in the refrigerator for up to 1 week.

MAKES 2 CUPS (1 LB/500 G)

Perfect Jasmine Rice

1½ cups (12 fl oz/375 ml) water
1 cup (7 0z/220 g) jasmine rice
1 Tbsp butter or olive oil, optional
½ tsp salt, optional

In a small saucepan with a lid, combine the water, rice, and the butter and/or salt, if using. Bring to a boil over high heat, then cover, reduce the heat to low, and simmer for 15 minutes. Keeping the lid on the pan, remove the pan from the heat and let steam for 10 minutes. Remove the pan lid, fluff with a fork, and serve.

SERVES 4–6

Basic Vinaigrette

1 Tbsp white wine vinegar or red wine vinegar
3–4 Tbsp extra-virgin olive oil
Salt and freshly ground pepper

In a jar, combine the vinegar with the oil and salt and pepper to taste. Cover and shake until well blended.

MAKES ¼ CUP (2 FL OZ/60 ML)

Simple Syrup

1 cup (8 fl oz/ 250 ml) water
1 cup (8 oz/250 g) sugar

In a small saucepan over medium-high heat, combine the water and sugar. Bring to a boil, stirring, until sugar has dissolved. Transfer to a container and let cool. Use right away, or cover and refrigerate for up to 2 weeks.

MAKES ABOUT 1½ CUPS (12 FL OZ/375 ML)

Easy Blueberry Syrup

2 cups (8 oz/250 g) blueberries
1 cup (11 fl oz/345 ml) maple syrup

In a small saucepan over medium heat, combine the blueberries and maple syrup. Bring to a simmer, then continue to simmer, stirring occasionally, until the blueberries start to release their juices, about 5 minutes. Serve warm, or let cool, cover, and refrigerate for up to 2 days. Rewarm before serving.

MAKES ABOUT 2½ CUPS (20 FL OZ/625 ML)

Bing Cherry Syrup

1 cup (7 oz/220 g) firmly packed light brown sugar
1 cup (8 oz/250 g) granulated sugar
¾ lb (375 g) large Bing cherries, pitted
1½ tsp almond extract

In a saucepan, combine both sugars. Add 2 cups (16 fl oz/ 500 ml) water and bring to a boil over high heat, stirring, until the sugar has dissolved. Continue to cook, uncovered, for 5 minutes. Add the cherries, reduce the heat to low, and simmer uncovered until the cherries are soft, 8–10 minutes. Stir in the almond extract and simmer for about 2 minutes longer to blend the flavors. Serve warm, or let cool, cover, and refrigerate for up to 2 days. Rewarm before serving.

MAKES ABOUT 2½ CUPS (20 FL OZ/625 ML)

Vanilla Whipped Cream

1 cup (8 fl oz/250 ml) heavy cream
1 Tbsp sugar, or more to taste
1 tsp pure vanilla extract

In the bowl of a mixer fitted with the whip attachment, add the cream, sugar to taste, and vanilla. Beat on medium-high speed until medium peaks form. Don't overwhip the cream, or it will become stiff and grainy. Serve right away, or cover with plastic wrap, refrigerate, and serve within 2 hours; fluff the cream with a whisk before serving.

MAKES ABOUT 2 CUPS (16 FL OZ/500 ML)

Dark Chocolate Sauce

4 oz (125 g) dark chocolate, coarsely chopped
½ cup (4 fl oz/125 ml) heavy cream

Place the chocolate in a large metal bowl and place it over (but not touching) a saucepan with barely simmering water. Warm, stirring often, until the chocolate melts. Remove from the heat and set aside.

In a small saucepan over medium heat, heat the cream until very hot but not quite simmering. Whisk the hot cream into the melted chocolate until smooth. Use right away, or cover and refrigerate until ready to use and warm gently before using.

MAKES ABOUT ¾ CUP (6 FL OZ/180 ML)

Candied Orange Peel

2 oranges
2 cups (1 lb/500 g) sugar

Using a vegetable peeler, remove the zest from each orange in long, wide strips. Using a small, sharp knife, trim away any white pith that remains on the zest, then cut the zest into thin strips.

Bring a saucepan three-fourths full of water to a boil over high heat. Add the zest strips and boil for 4 minutes. Drain and rinse with cold water.

In the same saucepan, combine the sugar with 1½ cups (12 fl oz/375 ml) water and the prepared zest. Bring to a simmer over medium-low heat and cook until the zest is soft and translucent, about 30 minutes. Remove from the heat and let the zest cool in the syrup. Using a slotted spoon or tongs, transfer the zest strips to a wire rack to dry; discard the syrup or reserve for another use. Use right away, or transfer to an airtight container and store at room temperature for up to 5 days.

MAKES ABOUT 1 CUP (3 OZ/90 G)

Index

weldonowen

1045 Sansome Street, Suite 100
San Francisco, CA 94111
www.weldonowen.com

Weldon Owen is a division of Bonnier Publishing USA

Weldon Owen, Inc.
President & Publisher Roger Shaw
SVP, Sales & Marketing Amy Kaneko
Finance & Operations Director Philip Paulick

Associate Publisher Amy Marr
Senior Editor Lisa Atwood

Creative Director Kelly Booth
Art Director Alexandra Zeigler
Senior Production Designer Rachel Lopez Metzger

Production Director Chris Hemesath
Associate Production Director Michelle Duggan

Imaging Manager Don Hill

Photographer John Kernick
Digital Tech/Photographer's Assistant Rizwan A. Alvi
Food Stylist Alison Attenborough
Food Stylist Assistants Alex Leonard,
Brett Regot, Karolina Wojcik
Prop Stylists Alistair Turnbull, Maya Rossi
Prop Stylists Assistants Kelsie Conley, Kate Donovan,
Layla Kenney, John Lingenfelter

Newlywed Entertaining
Conceived and produced by Weldon Owen, Inc.
In collaboration with Williams Sonoma, Inc.
3250 Van Ness Avenue, San Francisco, CA 94109

A Weldon Owen Production
Copyright © 2016 Weldon Owen Inc.
and Williams Sonoma, Inc.

All rights reserved, including the right of reproduction
in whole or in part in any form.

Printed and bound in China by 1010 International

First printed in 2016
10 9 8 7 6 5 4 3 2 1

Library of Congress Cataloging-in-Publication
data is available.

ISBN 13: 978-1-68188-140-9
ISBN 10: 1-68188-140-3

Acknowledgments
Weldon Owen wishes to thank the following people
for their generous support in producing this book:
Lesley Bruynesteyn, Pranavi Chopra, Kate Chynoweth,
Peggy Fallon, Gloria Geller, Dana Jacobi, Eve Lynch, Rachel Markowitz,
Alexis Mersel, Elizabeth Parson, Tori Ritchie, Sharon Silva,
Patricia Tompkins, Emely Vertiz, and Tamara White.

Photography Credits
All photographs by John Kernick except:
Masterfile, pages 18 and 35;
Offset, pages 111 and 229.